Devotions A-Z

by

Kenneth M. Lee

Life's Answers from God's Word

Copyright © 2016 by Kenneth M. Lee, Devotions A-Z; (1000 copies @ New Hanover Printing, Wilmington NC).
4ᵗʰ Edition -- Kindle Publishing
ISBN 9780971185050

Kenneth M. Lee
1382 Grandpa Lane
Loris SC 29569
kenlwor@gmail.com
: http://thedivineway.wordpress.com

About the Author: Kenneth Lee is retired and lives in Loris, South Carolina, U.S.A. His devotions have been published in *The Loris Scene, The Upper Room (for Christmas Eve of 1999), Penned from the Heart, The Secret Place,* and *The Daily Bread.* He has self-published three fiction books in the Marcia Lane Suspense series (a woman who gets stalked and becomes a Private Investigator): *Victim's Vengeance, Unveiled,* and *Jewel Time.*
His autobiography is *Persecuted But Not Forsaken,* and he published a sister book to *Devotions A-Z* entitled *God's Divine Help. Southern Devotions (with color photographs) is an accumulation of stories showing God's presence in society and nature,* 2023.

To order book(s), go to Amazon.com on the Internet.

All Bible Scripture References are from the King James Version of the Holy Bible and the New Schofield Reference Edition of the Holy Bible

This Book is for You

May you increase in the knowledge of God and Jesus Christ, be set free from any bondage, enjoy good health, and serve the Lord with joy.

The Lord is nigh unto all those who call upon him, to all who call upon him in truth. He will fulfill the desire of those who fear him; he also will hear their cry, and will save them.

Psalms 145:18-19

Table of Contents

Introduction

Welcome to *Devotions A-Z*. It is my sincere hope that you draw close to God as you read these devotions and prayers and apply them to your life.

The Bible is a guide for living, but its precepts, laws, and stories must be understood and practiced.

Devotions A-Z is a good place to start studying the Holy Scriptures. The scriptures referenced, and the devotions written are ones fundamental to the Judeo-Christian faith; however, the reader is encouraged to acquire an exhaustive concordance to the Bible, an expository, Hebrew and Greek Interlinear texts, and other translations of the Holy Scriptures. These resources are necessary to ascertain God's truth.

But all the studying in the world at this present time will not enable a person to find complete rest, peace, and happiness – in a world that has become polluted with weaponry, mass communication devices, and toxins. Until these devices are eliminated -- and toxins cleaned of land, sea, and air -- there will be little environmental peace.

Yet God has commanded us to be holy; neither shall ye defile the land.

As a young boy raised by my mother, who was raised on the Cherokee Indian Reservation, being holy, righteous, and reverent towards God, man, and the environment, went a long way towards finding peace and happiness. Learning about the herbs of the field and their natural remedies helped keep me physically well.

But having a full relationship with God the Father in Heaven is the ultimate answer for complete joy.

May God reveal Himself to you in this book. May he grant you peace, wisdom, and happiness -- and an understanding of just what he wants you to do. There is no greater joy -- than to serve the living God of the universe in truth, righteousness, and love.

Abandoned – Old Testament

And they took him, and cast him into a pit, and the pit was empty; there was no water in it.

Genesis 37: 24

Joseph was abandoned by his brothers and left in a pit to die until some merchantmen came along to lift him out.

Friends or family may abandon us, or even try to sell us, but being abandoned is a good time for drawing close to God.

Joseph prospered knowing God. He became a rich ruler in Egypt, and in due time, was reunited with his family.

The Bible says, For the Lord thy God is a merciful God, he will not forsake thee . . . (Deuteronomy 4:31).

Reading scripture, praying, and listening to God's word, helps us to know God never abandons us.

Dear Lord, I thank you for being here with me when I call upon your name. Forgive me if I have sinned, and bring me back into fellowship with family, friends, and believers. Amen.

Abandoned -- New Testament

Let your manner of life be without covetousness, and be content with such things as ye have; for he hath said, "I will never leave thee, nor forsake thee."
Hebrews 13:5

God is with us but it helps to call on his name to know he is with us.

I felt abandoned after my wife left me one day, but I awoke the next morning and went to the church building. In the middle of a hallway, someone exclaimed, "God is here."

Well, God is here, and God's Son Jesus is here also.

"Abide in me, and I in you," Jesus said in John 15:4.

So when feeling abandoned, consider Christ also as a friend who is here.

He said, "Ye are my friends, if ye do whatever I command you" (John 15:14).

Christ at one time was abandoned by his disciples, yet he remained faithful to God (Mark 14:50).

Dear Lord, I thank you for the fellowship in Christ Jesus who has died for my sin and wants to be my friend. May I share this good news with other people who feel abandoned. Amen.

Other Bible References: Psalms 68:5-6, 133:1, 145:18; Isaiah 41:10; John 6:37; 14:23.

Adultery – Old Testament

And David sent messengers, and took her; and she came in unto him, and he lay with her; for she was purified from her uncleanness: and she returned unto her house.

2 Samuel 11:4

David committed adultery with Bathsheba while his men were fighting a battle at Rabbah.

Perhaps if David would have been with his men, they would have won the battle -- and David would have won the battle over the lust of his flesh.

But when David saw Bathsheba bathing on a rooftop and asked her into his home, lust conceived.

God wants all of our attention on him rather than a temptation to sin (Exodus 19:3); otherwise, there will be discipline. David was confronted by Nathan the prophet about the sin and he went into deep mourning.

Consider reading Psalms 32 and 51 to see how David found God.

Dear Lord, Have mercy on me and forgive my sin. I humble myself from this sin of adultery. You are righteous. Restore this marriage by your mercy, forgiveness, and truth. Amen.

Adultery -- New Testament

And he saith unto them, "Whosoever shall put away his wife, and marry another, committeth adultery against her. And if a woman shall put away a husband, and marry another, she committeth adultery."
Mark 10:11-12

Divorcing a spouse commits adultery because a faithful commitment of togetherness has been made in front of a holy God -- and God expects us to fulfill our vows.

But Jesus takes the issue of adultery further and says, "That whosoever looketh on a woman to lust after her hath committed adultery with her already in his heart" (Matthew 5:28).

If adultery does occur, God has provided Jesus as a sacrifice for sin.

A woman, who was found in the act of adultery, was brought to Jesus for judgment, but Jesus did not condemn her (John 8:1-14).

He instead received her, and said, "Go, and sin no more."

Dear Father in Heaven, I come to you in humble confession and ask for forgiveness for my adulterous act. Restore this marriage I pray. Amen.

Other Bible References: Hosea 2:1; Corinthians 7:1-3; James 1:14-15.

Afraid – Old Testament

And Moses said unto the people, "Fear ye not, stand still, and see the salvation of the Lord, which he will show to you today."

Exodus 14:13

God is the God of comfort and protection but when the Israelites looked up and saw Pharaoh's army chasing them, they became terrified. Their leader Moses told them to be still – and see the salvation of the Lord.

The people waited -- and God held back the waters of the Red Sea while they traveled safely to the other side. But Pharaoh's approaching army was overwhelmed by the water.

The Bible says: God is our refuge and strength, a very present help in time of trouble (Psalms 46:1).

May we look to God to know he is in control and will guide us to comfort.

Consider reading the Exodus story, Psalms 31, 46, and Isaiah 51:1-16, to know God comforts His people.

Dear Lord, Your comfort is here and I trust You to help me. May I be still and know that you are a God of comfort. Amen.

Afraid – New Testament

The Lord is my helper, and I will not fear what men shall do unto me.

Hebrews 13:6

Much of our fear comes from man, who now has weaponry in the skies, terrorists on the streets, and deceivers in the marketplace. But the Bible advises us to fear God and not man.

It is God who has power to cast the soul into hell (Luke 12:5); therefore, we need to make peace with God.

Comfort from God comes through Jesus Christ by the confession of sin. Acceptance of Christ brings the Holy Spirit as our Comforter (John 14:26, 15:26).

The last thing we fear is death, but Christ has defeated death by his resurrection from the grave (1 Corinthians 15:54-57; Romans 8:35-39).

Dear Lord, I praise you for Jesus who takes away fear and sin. Christ is a Savior I can trust to give me peace. May I find comfort in your holy place of refuge. Amen.

Other Bible References: Psalms 27:1, 46:10, 56:3-4, 91:15-16; Proverbs 3:25; Isaiah 55:12; Romans 8:15, 10:13; John 14:26, 16:33; 2 Corinthians 1: 3-5; Hebrews 10:26-36; 1 Peter 3:14; 1 John 4:18.

Aging –Old Testament

And Moses was an hundred and twenty years old when he died; his eye was not dim, nor his natural force abated.
Deuteronomy 34:7

Moses was a man who looked good at his death, but he had actively worked for God in life.

He had walked up and down a mountain to receive God's commandments, crossed a sea to lead people to safety, and camped in a wilderness to worship God.

We should be so active, but if we are sitting around and not doing anything, we are slowly aging.

The proverb says, By much slothfulness the building decayeth, and through idleness of the hands, the house droppeth through (Ecclesiastes 10:18).

Our house may be deteriorating along with our body if we don't get up and work for God.

Sharing God's word of life is what keeps us going, such as Moses, who testified of God to the people before he died.

Dear Lord, I thank you for your presence here today. My body sometimes gets weak, but your spirit makes me strong. Amen.

And be renewed in the spirit of your mind. And that ye put on the new man, which after God is created in righteousness and true holiness.
Ephesians 4:23-24

Upon acceptance as Christ as Savior, the old is passed away and all things are new (2 Corinthians 5:17).

A ruler named Nicodemus wanted to know how to put off the old person and become born again. He asked Jesus, "How can a man be born when he is old? Can he enter the second time into his mother's womb, and be born?" (John 3:4).

Jesus said, (in the transliteration of the Greek language), "You must receive birth from above" (John 3:7).

That's what we need! Heavenly birth from above, which allows us to actively witness for the living God.

Consider reading Ephesians 4:22-32 for a renewal of your life.

Dear Father in Heaven, I thank you for the eternal life in Christ Jesus who is able to lift me up. Forgive my sins I pray through Christ and allow me to serve you in newness of spirit. Amen.

Other Bible References about Living a long life: Exodus 20:12; Deuteronomy 30:18; Job 11:13-20; Psalms 103; Proverbs 3:1-3; Luke 10:25; John 3:16, 7:40; Romans 6-10; Colossians 3:9-17; 1 Peter 3:10; Hebrews 6:12; Prayer for old age, Psalms 71.

Alcohol – Old Testament

". . . neither have ye drunk wine or strong drink: that ye might know that I am the Lord your God."
Deuteronomy 29:6

Abstaining from drinking fermented beverages brings us closer to know the Lord because our bodies are not diluted with alcohol.

But it took a wilderness experience for the Israelites to realize God was their sole provider.

The Bible says, Wine is a mocker, strong drink is raging: and whosoever is deceived thereby is not wise (Proverbs 20:1).

The wisest thing we can do is give our bodies' nutritious food and pure drink; then we can begin to serve the Lord in sincerity and truth.

Dear Lord, I trust you to keep me in the right place around the right people. May my body be purged of alcohol so I can be healthy for your service. Amen.

Alcohol -- New Testament

"Verily I say unto you, I will drink no more of the fruit of the vine until that I drink it new in the kingdom of God."
Mark 14:25

Jesus would not allow himself to drink vinegar for pleasure until he had performed the will of his Father in Heaven. In other words, work for God took priority in his life.

Knowing God's work has priority over our lives, and we should abstain from drinking excess alcohol.

The Bible says drunkards do not inherit the kingdom of God (1 Corinthians 6:10). The New Testament further instructs us to be not drunk with wine, in which is excess, but be filled with the Spirit (Ephesians 5:18).

The temptation to drink alcohol may be strong but God gives us the victory over temptation through Jesus Christ, who has defeated the lust of the flesh (read Galatians 5: 17-24).

Dear Lord, May I abstain from alcohol and learn more about God's word, which gives me strength and life. Grant me a new life in Christ Jesus. Amen.

Other Bible References: Isaiah 56-58; Psalms 104:15; Proverbs 23:29-30; John 6:53-56, 7:37; Romans 6:1-13; 1 Timothy 5:23; 1 Peter 2:11.

And it came to pass, as soon as he came nigh unto the camp, that he saw the calf, and the dancing; and Moses anger waxed hot, and he cast the tables out of his hands, and brake them beneath the mount.

Exodus 32:19

Moses got so angry at seeing the people worship a false idol that he threw down the tablets of stone containing God's Ten Commandments and they broke.

That only made matters worse, because he had to go back up the mountain and make two more tablets.

When we see things that make us angry, turning to God helps us find peace and guidance. The Bible says, Cease from anger, and forsake wrath, fret not thyself in any wise to do evil (Psalms 37:8).

But God does get angry: He is angry with the wicked everyday (Psalms 7:11). He had Moses divide the golden calf idolaters from those people who were on the Lord's side--and three thousand idolaters were slain.

May we fear God enough to be on his side of anger.

Dear Lord, I pray you take this anger away so that I can have peace. I look to you for the right and wise thing to do. Amen.

And they come to Jerusalem: and Jesus went into the temple, and began to cast out them that sold and bought in the temple, and overthrew the tables of the moneychangers, and the seats of them that sold doves.

Mark 11:15

Jesus got angry at seeing God's holy temple being made a marketplace for the buying and selling of sacrificial offerings.

We often get angry at seeing unrighteousness. Children may become disobedient, people may trespass against us, or leaders may become corrupt, but this is a good time for seeking God's wisdom; otherwise, we could become the victims of anger. The scribes and chief priests conspired to hurt Jesus; so he left town (Mark 11:18).

If our anger is unjustified, Jesus says we are in danger of judgment and we should make peace with the adversary (Matthew 5:22-26).

Possibly the best advice comes from the Book of Ephesians: Be ye angry, and sin not; let not the sun go down upon your wrath (Ephesians 4:26).

Dear Lord, It makes me upset to see unrighteousness, but You are the great judge, and I know you will fix this situation. Grant me wisdom to know what to do. Amen.

Other Bible References: Exodus 32:22; Psalms 2:11-12; Proverbs 15:1, 19:11; Matthew 5:12; Colossians 3:8; Philippians 4:7.

Argument (Rebukement) – Old Testament

Thou shalt not hate thy brother in thine heart; thou shalt surely rebuke thy neighbor, and not allow sin upon him.
Leviticus 19:17

Confronting someone about a sin may lead to an argument, but we love our brothers and sisters enough to correct them if they are sinning.

The Bible says, Rebuke a wise man, and he will love thee (Proverbs 9:8); Open rebuke is better than secret love (Proverbs 27:5); Iron sharpeneth iron, so a man sharpeneth the countenance of his friend (Proverbs 27:17).

However, before we correct someone, we should be wise to search out God's scriptures: it may be that we are the ones who need corrected.

In contrast to those proverbs, there are people that should not be rebuked. Answer not a fool according to his folly, lest thou also be like unto him (Proverbs 26:4); and, Rebuke not a scorner, lest he hate thee (Proverbs 9:8).

Dear Lord, May I refrain from debates and disputes, yet if I must argue, may I do so in the spirit of brotherhood and righteousness. Amen.

Argument - New Testament

I told you, and you believed not; the works that I do in my Father's name, they bear witness of me.

John 10:25

Jesus found himself in the middle of arguments on several occasions: he argued for new Sabbath day regulations -- and him being the Son of God.

If we are committed to God, we will be arguing for righteous principles.

The Bible advises us to rebuke liars and hypocrites sharply, that they may be sound in the faith (read Titus 1:9-- 2:15).

Arguments take place daily, in courtrooms, business offices, homes, and on playgrounds. These are good opportunities to proclaim righteousness but also witness for God.

But the Apostle Paul says to do all things without murmurings and disputings, that ye may be blameless and harmless, the sons of God without rebuke . . . (Philippians 2:14-15).

Dear Lord, It upsets me to argue, but at times, this has to be done. May I receive the strength and facts to argue righteously with you as witness. Amen.

Other Bible References: Psalms 39:11; Mark 8:31-33; 1 Timothy 5:1.

And he believed in the Lord; and he counted it to him for righteousness.

Genesis 15:6

Abraham believed in the Lord because he received a vision that came true: he inherited land and a family.

We might also receive a vision from God that comes true, if we know God.

But obtaining God's vision is not without trials and troubles. For Abraham, a famine occurred and he had to travel to Egypt to find food. Furthermore, Abraham's wife, Sarah, mocked the suggestion they would have a child, and she sent away the bondwoman, Hagar, who had birthed Abraham's son, Ishmael. And Abraham was grieved.

Satan will do anything to stop us from obtaining God's blessings, but when God ordains something, it will come true, by belief.

The Bible says, "The Lord of hosts hath sworn, saying, Surely as I have thought, so shall it come to pass, and as I have purposed, so shall it stand," (Isaiah 14:24).

Dear Lord, I believe you are here when I call on your name, and you will perform that which you have shown me. May I be a faithful servant who carries out your mission for life. Amen.

Jesus said unto her, "I am the resurrection, and the life; he that believeth in me, though he were dead, yet shall he live."

John 11:25

Believing in Christ frees us from the fear of death and the bondage of sin.

For he hath made him, who knew no sin, to be sin for us, that we might be made the righteousness of God in him (2 Corinthians 5:21).

It's up to us to believe, but normally some tragedy takes place before we call on Jesus.

A nobleman's son was at the point of death, and the nobleman went to find Jesus.

Jesus told the man the son would live, if only he believed. When the nobleman returned home, servants met him on the way and confirmed the boy was alive (John 4:46-54).

Many people saw the miracles Jesus performed and they believed (John 2:23). Jesus raised the lame, opened the eyes of the blind, loosened the tongues of the mute, and forgave sin.

God's powers are with us -- when we believe.

John the Baptist told the Levites and priests, "Behold, the lamb of God, who taketh away the sin of world" (John 1:29).

Dear God, I believe in the resurrection of Christ to take away my sins and give me salvation. Amen.

Other Bible References: Exodus 4:4-5; Mark 9:23; John 3:16, 6:47, 10:37-38, Chapter 14; Acts 16:31; Romans 10:9; Ephesians 1:3-23; Hebrews 11:6.

Building -- Old Testament

Make thee an ark of gopher wood; rooms shalt thou make in the ark, and shalt pitch it within and without with pitch.
Genesis 6:14

God instructed Noah to build an ark because a catastrophic flood was coming to remove all the evil from the earth.

The ark would have a big door, window, and it would be three stories high -- to hold all of Noah's family and pairs of all known animals.

But when God builds things, he builds them just right.

The Bible says, "Except the Lord build the house, they labor in vain that build it; except the Lord keep the city, the watchman waketh but in vain," (Psalms 127:1).

May we look to the Lord for building shelter and transportation but also our spiritual lives around His Word of truth. God designed his Word to give us a foundation for a good lives.

He will keep us safe as he did Noah, who found grace in the eyes of the Lord and was saved from the flood.

Dear Father in Heaven, May I build according to your plan and make a sure foundation. Thank you for your Word of life. Amen.

Building -- New Testament

"In my Father's house are many mansions . . . .."
John 14:2

A good place to start building a life with Jesus is by reading the 14th Chapter of the Book of John and knowing there is a place in heaven reserved for you.

Jesus says, ". . . no man cometh to the Father, but by me" (John 14:6).

After receiving Jesus, lust and sin are defeated (Ephesians 4:21-24); and a new life of righteousness begins (2 Corinthians 5:17).

Our lives become complete when the love of Jesus dwells in us and the Holy Spirit blesses those around us.

Our feet walk with grace, our words are seasoned with truth, and our actions show mercy.

Dear God, I praise you for being here and building my faith in Jesus. May I complete the work you show me, and may I build using the right materials by faith and trust. Amen.

Other Biblical References: Matthew 7:24, 17:18; 1 Corinthians 3:9-17.

Children – Old Testament

And ye shall teach them your children, speaking of them when thou sittest in thine house, and when thou walkest by the way, when thou liest down, and when thou riseth up.
Deuteronomy 11:19

God wants us to tell our children about His statutes but also about how he delivered his people from slavery: With a mighty hand, and an outstretched arm, he brought them out of bondage (Deuteronomy 28:6).

Teaching children to fear and respect God will multiply their days upon earth (Deut. 11:21). However, children will need discipline.

The Bible says, Withhold not correction from a child . . . (Proverbs 23:13); the rod and reproof give wisdom, but a child left to himself, bringeth his mother to shame (Proverbs 29:15).

God gives us instruction on how to raise children. It's up to us to apply it and be reverent.

Dear Lord, Thank you for being here and helping me raise my children. Bless us as a family Lord, have mercy on us, and keep us together. Amen.

Children --New Testament

And ye fathers, provoke not your children to wrath: but bring them up in the nurture and admonition of the Lord.
Ephesians 6:4

God wants us to encourage our children and not be angry at them. That means to speak positively and show them the right way to do things.

The Bible says, And the servant of the Lord must not strive, but be gentle unto all men, apt to teach, patient (2 Timothy 2:24).

Children need to see our patience. They need to see our wisdom, and they need to see God in all that we do, because they will imitate our actions.

Consider reading Bible stories to children and attending church where they can interact with other kids.

Jesus, as a young child, was in the temple daily learning about God and gaining wisdom.

Dear Lord, Keep us together in the love and mercy of Jesus, who died for our sins. I will encourage my child daily with your help. Amen.

Other Bible References: Psalms 119:9; Proverbs 10:1, 13:24, 20:7, 22:6, 15.

When I kept silence, my bones waxed old through my roaring all the day long.

Psalms 32:3

King David is talking about his pain of keeping silent about his sin.

Our bones will become old and pains will exist if we don't confess sin.

The Bible says, He that covereth his sins shall not prosper, but whoso confesseth and forsaketh them shall have mercy (Proverbs 28:13).

God wants us to confess sins so we can have mercy and life, and God is faithful to forgive our sins when we bow to him in confession (2 Chronicles 7:14).

Dear God, "Have mercy upon me, O God, according to Thy loving kindness: according unto the multitude of Thy tender mercies blot out my transgressions. Wash me thoroughly from mine iniquity, cleanse me from my sin. For I acknowledge my transgressions and my sin is ever before me;" (Psalms 51:1-3). Amen.

Confession -- New Testament

If we confess our sins, he is faithful and just to forgive us our sins, and to cleanse us from all unrighteousness.
1 John 1:9

Before a confession of sin can take place, there must be an acknowledgment of sin. (An action has been compared with the law of God, and a transgression has occurred.)

Only a holy God can completely redeem sin. This is why God sent His Son Jesus to earth in the form of a sinless man from his virgin Mother Mary to be a perfect sacrifice for sin.

Consider talking to God in private prayer when sin begins to overflow. Jesus said to go to the Father in secret, and He will reward you openly (Matthew 6:6).

The Bible also says: That if thou shalt confess with thy mouth the Lord Jesus, and shalt believe in thine heart that God that raised him from the dead, thou shalt be saved (Romans 10:9).

Dear God, I bow down before you in humble confession. Please forgive me. I acknowledge my transgression and commit myself to your righteous ways. Thank you for Jesus who died for me. Amen.

Other Bible References: Matthew 10:32; Romans 14:11-12.

"Have not I commanded thee? Be strong and of good courage; be not afraid, neither be thou dismayed; for the Lord thy God is with thee wherever thou goest."
                                                        Joshua 1:9

After the death of Moses, Joshua assumed command of the Israelites and received confidence from the Lord to lead the people across the Jordan River to the land of promise.

But Joshua had known God from when he was a young man: he had worshipped in the tabernacle and saw him in a cloudy pillar (Ex. 33:11).

We should be so intimate with God, and we should know that God is our confidence. The Bible says, For the Lord shall be thy confidence, and keep thy foot from being taken (Proverbs 3:26).

But if sin is in our lives, we do not have God's confidence -- we have his condemnation (see Joshua 23:16).

The Israelites were defeated in a battle at Kadesh-Barnea because of doubting God (Numbers 14).

Moses had told the people, "Go not up, for the Lord is not among you; that ye be not smitten before your enemies" (Numbers 14:42).

But later after repentance, and following Joshua, who had God's confidence, the Israelites crossed the Jordan River and entered the land of promise.

Dear Lord, You are my confidence, and not man. I put you first in my life to achieve great things for your glory. Amen.

Confidence -- New Testament

Jesus answered and said unto him, "If a man loves me, he will keep my words; and my Father will love him, and we will come in unto him, and make our abode with him."
John 14:23

Having Jesus and God in our lives gives us great confidence: God is an advocate for our sins, and Jesus is the propitiation for them (1 John 2:1-2).

When we abide in Jesus and perform his sayings, then whatever we ask, it shall be done (John 15:7).

Jesus intercedes for us (Hebrews 7:25), and the Holy Spirit also intercedes according to the will of God (Romans 8:26).

This is great confidence.

Prayer bolsters our confidence. God shows us what to do, where to go, how to get there, and how to get things done — before it all takes place. And we know that what God purposes - -will come true.

Beloved, if our heart condemn us not, then we have confidence toward God (1 John 3:21).

Dear Lord, Thank You for giving me confidence through Christ Jesus. I can do all things through Christ who strengthens me. Amen.

Other Bible References: Psalms 118:6; Proverbs 14:16; Micah 7:5; Mark 9:23; John 15:1-6; Philippians 4:13; Psalm for Confidence, Psalms 3; and Triumphant Faith, Psalm 27.

The proud have had me greatly in derision, yet have I not declined from thy law.

Psalms 119:51

Satan's desire is to keep a person constantly confused, but knowing God's law rejects moral confusion: His statutes are right.

The Bible says, Thou shalt keep, therefore, his statutes, and his commandments, which I command thee this day, that it may go well with thee (Deuteronomy 4:40).

But many of us are stubborn, which may cause us to flee seven ways before enemies, be consumed with madness, and have sorrow of mind (read Deuteronomy 28:15-68).

Consider humbling yourself to God when confused, and remember, God is always in control.

The simplicity of life's requirement might be summed up in Micah 6:8: "What does the Lord require of thee but do to justice, love mercy, and walk humbly with thy God?"

Dear Father in Heaven, I thank you for your truth, for having a stable mind, and knowing right from wrong. May I humble myself under your great hand so that I am at peace. Amen.

Confusion -- New Testament

Wherefore, it is also contained in the scriptures, Behold, I lay in Zion a chief corner stone, elect, precious: and he that believeth on him shall not be confounded.

1 Peter 4:6

Believing in Jesus eliminates religious confusion because he is a total sacrifice for man's sins (Hebrews 10:1-14). He eliminates worldly confusion because he said the devil was a liar from the beginning (John 8:12-59). And he eliminates personal confusion because he saves us from sin and gives us security upon death.

We are instructed to be sober-minded (1 Thessalonians 5:4-11). Scripture also says, That we henceforth be no more children, tossed to and fro, and carried about with every wind of doctrine . . . But, speaking the truth in love . . . (Ephesians 4:14-15).

When burdened with confusion, search out the truth, for the truth makes a person free (John 8:32).

Man has made many devices and tried to distort truth, but we are encouraged to remain strong and employ a shield of faith against the works of the devil (Ephesians 6:10-20).

Dear Father in Heaven, I put my trust in you to reject confusion. May I rest in truth. Amen.

Other Bible References: Psalms 71:24; Proverbs 8:20, 24:10; Mark 12:29-31, 13:22; John 3:11; 1 Corinthians 1:26-30, 14:33; Romans 14:22-23; Philippians 4:1; Titus 2; Revelation 12:9; The Simplicity of Christ: 2 Corinthians 11:3.

And David said to Saul, 'Let no man's heart fail because of him; thy servant will go and fight with this Philistine."
1 Samuel 17:32

David had little fear of fighting the giant Goliath, because David knew God, and he had already killed a lion and bear.

So when Goliath threatened David, David responded by invoking God's name and slinging a stone at Goliath's forehead, and Goliath went down.

When there are threatening giants in our lives, we should invoke God's name for protection.

The Bible says, Through God we shall do valiantly; for he it is he who shall tread down our enemies (Psalms 60:12).

God is a partner we can count trust to defeat the enemy.

Dear Lord, With you, all things are indeed possible. Strengthen me to be courageous for your sake. Amen.

But Peter and John answered and said unto them, "Whether it is right in the sight of God to hearken unto you more than unto God, judge ye."

Acts 4:19

The Apostles showed great courage talking back to a Sanhedrin council despite being threatened with jail and beatings for preaching Jesus as Savior.

Testifying about Christ has it dangers, and Jesus confirms this when he says, "Whosoever will come after me, let him deny himself, and take up his cross, and follow me (Mark 8:34). In other words, there is the constant threat of dying.

Each of us who believes in Christ sacrifices a life of personal desire to fulfill God's desire.

The Apostles turned to God in prayer. "And now, Lord, behold their threatenings; and grant unto thy servants, that with all boldness they may speak thy word" (Acts 4:29).

When faced with fear, consider calling on God in prayer -- and Jesus -- for courage and strength.

Know Jesus has defeated the devil.

The Apostle Paul said, "I can do all things through Christ who strengthens me" (Philippians 4:13).

Dear Lord, Your presence here encourages me and I thank you in advance for defeating the enemy by righteousness and truth. Have mercy on me I pray. Amen.

Other Bible References: Psalms 27:14, 31: 24; John 16:33; 1 Corinthians 16:13; Ephesians 6:10.

And she sat apart from him, and lifted up her voice, and wept.

Genesis 21:16

Hagar is crying because her child is dying of thirst. She has walked off a short distance so she wouldn't see his death.

But God arrives and tells her he has heard the voice of the lad, and he shows her a well for water.

God knew the sad condition of the child and Hagar, and he knows our situation.

The Bible says, God is nigh unto those who are of a broken heart, and saveth such as be of a contrite spirit (Psalms 34:18).

Sad situations are good times for being close to God.

He will comfort us by his presence, and if we listen, encourage us to get stronger.

Dear Father in Heaven, I thank you for being close to my tears. Comfort me, and restore my strength I pray. Amen.

Crying -- New Testament

Jesus wept.

John 11:35

Jesus cried because his friend Lazarus has died.

But he didn't weep for long, because he wanted to show the power and glory of God.

Jesus went to the cave and ordered Lazarus to come forth, and Lazarus shed his grave-clothes.

Death of a loved one, or a sad circumstance, may make us weep, but it's also a good time to witness of God's presence.

When tears flow and life seems sad, look for Jesus in the midst.

The Bible says the lamb Jesus is in the midst of the throne . . . and shall lead them to fountains of living waters, and God shall wipe away all tears from their eyes (Revelation 7:17).

The Bible also says, Blessed are they that mourn, for they shall be comforted (Matthew 5:4).

Dear Father in Heaven, I thank you for being here amidst my tears, and I praise you for Jesus who gives me strength to live for your sake. Amen.

Other Bible References: Job 16:16-17; Psalms 6:8-9, 30:3, 126:5; Joel 2:12; James 4:8-10; Revelation 7:1, 21:4.

And it came to pass after these things, Joshua, the son of Nun, the servant of the Lord, died, being one hundred and ten years old.

Joshua 24:29

Before Joshua died, he testified of God's saving presence in front of the leaders of Israel and recollected the events of the past that had led to the people's freedom (Joshua 24:1-13).

We might also give testimony about God's presence before we die, but if we have differences with God, now is a good time for acknowledging them and asking forgiveness.

The Bible says, "For in death there is no remembrance of thee; in the grave who shall give thee thanks?" (Psalms 6:5).

Being forgiven by God allows us to freely testify of his presence. Friends and family can be saved by our testimonies, and they might be encouraged to follow God's way.

Dear Heavenly Father, Thank you for life, and I testify of your saving presence. Grant me mercy, peace, and rest. Amen.

For God so loved the world, that he gave his only begotten Son, that whosoever believeth in Him should not perish, but have everlasting life.

John 3:16

Jesus overcomes death by his resurrection from the grave, but many people have trouble believing.

The Apostle Thomas wanted to see the nail prints and the blood of Christ's body. When he saw, he believed (John 20:25-29).

God forbid us to see wounds and blood before we believe in the risen Christ.

When the shadows become longer, the body moves slower, and the vision blurs, Jesus is still here to give us life.

Jesus says, "I am the resurrection and the life: he that believeth in me, though he were dead, yet shall he live. And whosoever liveth and believeth in me shall never die. Believest thou this?" (John 11:25-26).

Dear Lord, I praise you for sending Jesus to free me from the pains of death and give me peace. I believe in the Holy Ghost, the forgiveness of sins, and life everlasting. Amen.

Other Bible References: Genesis 3:19; Psalms 88:10-12; John 11:25; Romans 6:11; Ephesians 2:5, 5:14.

Debt – Old Testament

... Thy servant my husband is dead; and thou knowest that thy servant did fear the Lord: and the creditor is come to take my two sons to be bondmen.

1 Kings 4:1

A woman was in monetary debt, and about to lose her two sons; so she called on a man of God, Elisha, for help.

Elisha told her to go home and divide what little oil she had and put it in separate containers to sell.

Wisdom suggests we might divide what little we have to make it last longer, or sell something to pay off a debt.

But the only debt we should have is praising God every day and witnessing for him.

Psalms 23 tells us to trust the Lord for our needs: "The Lord is my shepherd, I shall not want [lack]" (Psalms 23:1).

If we have borrowed a tangible asset, we don't want to be known as a wicked people who don't pay their debts (Psalms 37:21); so we should pay what we owe.

The writer of Ecclesiastes gives us good advice about borrowing money: Better is it that thou shouldest not vow, then that thou shouldest vow and not pay (Eccl. 5:5).

Dear Father in Heaven, Please show me the way to repay this debt. May I never borrow again. I trust you to supply my needs. Amen.

Debt -- New Testament

"The servant, therefore, fell down, and worshiped him, saying, 'Lord, have patience with me, and I will pay thee all'."
Matthew 18:26

Jesus tells a story about a poor servant owing money to his master and the master requiring payment.

The poor servant bowed down before the master and asked for mercy – and he received it.

Maybe the servant was too poor to make a payment.

But the same poor servant had a man who owed him money – and he would not forgive.

The servant's lord found out about this, saying the servant had been forgiven earlier; yet would not forgive a man who owed him.

So the servant was sent to his creditors' tormentors – and he would have to work to pay off his debt.

Part of the Lord's prayer says, "And forgive us our debts, as we forgive our debtors" (Matthew 6:12). If we ask mercy from God, we should show mercy to others.

But if we are in debt to sin, Christ's death on the cross has paid the price.

Upon confession and redemption of sin, we are free to serve and worship the living God (Romans 3:24-26; 1 Peter 1"18-19).

Dear Lord, I ask for patience paying off this debt, and I promise never to get in monetary debt again. I am reminded to witness for you and Christ, who frees me from sin. Amen.

Other Bible References: Psalms 37:21; Proverbs 22:7; Romans 3:23-24, 13:8.

Devil – Old Testament

Now there was a day when the Sons of God came to present themselves before the Lord, and Satan came also among them.

Job 1:6

Job had a big family, which liked to feast and have parties.

Job knew they were probably sinning, because he would go and offer burnt sacrifices to God for them.

But that did not help the children, for God's judgment would take place and Job lost family, cattle, house, and health.

Had Job been with his family to guide and protect, possibly this tragedy would never have happened.

Satan is ever present in the world.

But God has power over Satan. It is up to us to obey him and stay separate from sin.

The Psalmist says, Because thou hast made the Lord, who is my refuge, even the Most High, thy habitation, there shall no evil befall thee, neither shall any plague come nigh thy dwelling (Psalms 91:9-10).

When Satan comes around, stay around God's throne for victory, but it may mean to repent in ashes and dust like Job.

Dear Father in Heaven, Thank you for having power over the devil. When Satan comes around, I look to you for help and protection. Have mercy on me Lord. Amen.

Devil -- New Testament

Be sober, be vigilant; because your adversary the devil, as a roaring lion, walketh about, seeking whom he may devour, whom resist steadfast in the faith, knowing that the same afflictions are accomplished in our brethren that are in the world.

1 Peter 5:8-9

In order to resist the devil, we must understand the traits of the devil:: he lies, cheats, steals, murders, and deceives. He is presumptuous, prideful, malignant, wise, envious, and covetous.

The good news is that Christ has defeated the devil.

When tempted to sin by the devil in the wilderness, Jesus quoted God's word and said God could not be tempted. He told the devil to go away.

Christ further conquered the devil when he took the people's sins to the cross and put them to death.

There was a devil in a young man in Matthew 17. He was being thrown into fire and water, but Jesus confronted the evil spirit, and it left.

Christ gets rid of devils.

The power of Christ in holiness, righteousness, and resurrection from the dead, defeats devils.

Dear Lord, I confront the devil in the power of Jesus Christ and your righteousness, but I am also humble enough to let you drive him away. Amen.

Other Bible References, Genesis 3:14; Isaiah 14:15; Zechariah 3:1; Matthew 17:15; Mark 12:17; Romans 16:20; 1 Timothy 3:7; Ephesians 4:27; James 4:7.

And as he passed over Penuel the sun rose upon him, and he halted upon his thigh.

Genesis 32:31

Jacob became disabled when he failed to bless God.

We may become disabled from failing to bless God.

Or possibly, we are disabled from birth or have suffered a tragic accident.

But we are still whole in the spirit to glorify God, if have received him into our lives.

Glorifying God can be done in many ways: testifying about God's presence, writing about God's glory, or using what bodily members we have to be productive and faithful.

The Bible says God formed Jacob for His purpose (Isaiah 43:1-13).

And God has formed us for his purpose – despite physical limitations.

Jacob was made whole in his faith, and he visited brother Esau with blessings.

Dear Lord, I am complete with you, fully able to pray and serve. Have mercy upon me, and may you be glorified in all that I do. Amen.

. . . There was given to me a thorn in the flesh, the messenger of Satan to buffet me, lest I should be exalted above measure.

2 Corinthians 12:7

The Apostle Paul felt his disability kept him humble.

Being disabled physically keeps us humble, because we move slower and feel pain.

An impotent man lay by healing waters but there was no one to help him enter the pool, until Jesus came along and said, "Arise, take up thy bed, and walk" (John 5:1-9).

Jesus gives us strength, because of his faith.

The man believed in Jesus, and walked into the pool.

Other sick, disabled, and impotent people came to Jesus and were healed (Matthew 15: 30).

But if we don't know Jesus, we need to learn about him to complete our faith.

Disabled in the world, but able in God to do exceedingly above all we think or ask when we yield our members to him (Ephesians 3:14-21).

God has given us the spirit of grace through Jesus to bear disabilities (2 Corinthians 12:9); Jesus intercedes for our suffering (Hebrews 4:14-16).

Dear Heavenly Father, Everyday is difficult in this body, but you fill me with the spirit. May I use my body to produce good work and testify of your strength and grace. Amen.

Other Bible Reference Scriptures: Psalms 25, 88, 100:3, 138:8; Isaiah 43:7, 53:5; Matthew 18:8; Luke 5:24-25; John 9:3, 17:23; Romans 8:26; 2 Corinthians 12:12-26; Colossians 2:9-10; Hebrews 4:15, 7:25.

. . . And he requested for himself that he might die, and said, "It is enough!"

1 Kings 19:4

Elijah was discouraged because King Ahab's wife Jezebel was seeking to kill him, so he walked out a day's distance in the desert and sat under a juniper tree hoping to die.

But God sent an angel to touch Elijah and told him to get up, eat, and continue on the journey.

We may feel so discouraged we want to die, but God is here.

In the heat of the day, under the shade of the Almighty, we might hear the words that give us new life: "Arise, eat, and continue on the journey."

Dear Lord, I am encouraged by your presence here. Let me be faithful to achieve that which you want me to do in my life. Amen.

Discouragement -- New Testament

And saith unto them, "My soul is exceeding sorrowful unto death: tarry ye here, and watch."
Mark 14:34

Jesus was discouraged because the time was drawing near for him to die for the people's sins, and he found his disciples sleeping at a time when soldiers would soon come to arrest him.

But he looked to God for encouragement: he walked off a short distance and bowed in prayer.

We can become discouraged in a world of poverty, sickness, war, and tragedy, but God is still here for encouragement.

He gave Jesus the strength to complete his calling, and he gives us strength to achieve great things for his name's sake.

We are also advised to encourage each other (Hebrews 10:25).

Dear Lord, I am discouraged about the events taking place around me; but I know you are in charge. You are my strength to perform good works and glorify your name. Amen.

Other Bible References: Deuteronomy 1:21; Numbers 32:7; John 10:10; Colossians 3:21; James 5:13-16.

Divorce – Old Testament

. . . then let him write her a bill of divorcement, and give it in her hand, and send her out of his house.
Deuteronomy 24:1

Divorce was permitted in the Old Testament when the man felt his wife was unfavorable towards him.

But the man had been given power over the woman in the beginning (Genesis 3:16); and he had the authority to void or accept her words (Numbers 30:6-8).

Divorce between a man and a woman was not meant to be: the man and woman were created in God's image to be together and multiply on the face of the earth (Genesis 1:17).

Before getting divorced, make sure a relationship with God is intact: we do not want to be divorced from God.

The Lord our God is one Lord (Deuteronomy 6:4).

Dear Lord, You are the one I should truly be married to, but I also pray for my spouse to come to know your love, mercy, and fellowship. Amen.

Divorce -- New Testament

But if the unbelieving depart, let him depart. A brother or a sister is not under bondage in such cases; but God hath called unto peace.

1 Corinthians 7:15

The Apostle Paul tries to justify the separation of an unbelieving spouse by saying there should be peace.

But marriage is a bond -- and Christ Jesus says a spouse should not divorce but in the case of fornication (Matthew 5:32).

Jesus further says, "What therefore God hath joined together, let man not put asunder"; (Matthew 19:6).

Scripture encourages us to be kind one to another, tenderhearted, forgiving one another, even as God, for Christ's sake, hath forgiven you (Ephesians 4:32).

Nevertheless, problems do occur within a marriage.

Pray for a separated mate to find Jesus. Regardless of what happens in a domestic marriage, Jesus is a mate for life.

Wherefore, my brethren, ye also are become dead to the law by the body of Christ; that ye should be married to another, even to him who is raised from the dead, that we should bring forth fruit unto God (Romans 7:4).

Dear Lord, If I have sinned, forgive me of sin and let me reconcile with you. I love you Lord, and I hope my mate loves you and finds your mercy. Amen.

Drugs – Old Testament

"Is not this the fast that I have chosen -- to loose the bands of wickedness, to undo the heavy burdens, and to let the oppressed go free, and that ye break every yoke?"
Isaiah 58:6

Breaking the drug habit requires something be put in its place, like faith in the living God. He is able to give spiritual joy in life and keep the body nutritionally healthy.

Read Isaiah 56-58 to learn about how separation to God through fasting and Sabbath day holiness brings blessings.

In another reading, a psalmist said he called on the name of the Lord and was saved from death; he was brought low -- but the Lord helped him ((Psalm 116:4-8).

When the body becomes free of drugs, and the mind fully dependent on God, then joy will indeed break forth as the morning sun, and good health will flourish as a tree besides living waters (Isaiah 58: 8).

Dear Father in Heaven, You are the way for life and I commit my way to you. I confess my inadequacies and solely trust you to provide me peace, happiness, and the work I need for a prosperous life. Amen.

Drugs – New Testament

And they that are Christ's have crucified the flesh with the affections and lust.

Galatians 5: 24

Christ Jesus gives us power over the temptation to take drugs because he has crucified the lusts of the flesh, risen from the dead, and intercedes for us.

When a temptation comes to take a drug, look to Christ who sits on the right hand side of God (Hebrews 1:3). The devil has been defeated, but it takes our faith in the living Christ to rebuke and send him away.

Our bodies should be used for God's purpose and service (1 Corinthians 6:20; Romans 12).

Consider also reading the 1st and 2nd chapter of Ephesians to see Christ's power over fleshly lusts.

God is faithful, who will not suffer you to be tempted above that ye are able, but will, with the temptation, also make a way to escape, that ye may be able to bear it (1 Corinthians 10:13).

Dear Lord, I confess my sin and call on your name for help. Have mercy on me and renew me in the right spirit to love Jesus in body, mind, and soul. I can do all this through Christ who strengthens me. Amen.

Other Bible References: 2 Chronicles 7:14; 1 Corinthians 9:27; 2 Peter 1:7; Nutrition: Romans 14.

And he humbled thee, and suffered thee to hunger, and fed thee with manna, which thou knewest not, that he might make thee know that man doth not live by bread only, but by every word that proceedeth out of the mouth of the Lord doth man live.

Deuteronomy 8:3

God caused the Hebrews to hunger temporarily so they would learn that man does not live by bread alone -- but by the word of God.

In times of famine, we might also take some biblical advice from the psalmist: Trust in the Lord, and do good; so shalt thou dwell in the land, and verily thou shalt be fed (Psalms 37:3).

Consider also the words of Agur in the Book of Proverbs: "Remove far from me vanity and lies; give me neither poverty nor riches; feed me with food convenient for me" (Proverbs 30:8).

A gift from God is to be able to work and eat, but we are also expected to acknowledge his presence.

Dear Father in Heaven, I thank you for bread from earth, but I also thank you for bread from heaven. Your Word feeds me the wisdom I need to work and testify of your saving presence. Amen.

Hast thou faith? Have it to thyself before God. Happy is he that condemneth not himself in that thing which he alloweth.

Romans 14:22

If you have not prayed before eating food from the earth, you are not acknowledging the very God who grows food.

And that can be trouble.

The New Testament of Jesus Christ, has allowed us to consume foods that were not allowed in the Old Testament: it is Christ who has power over this by his virgin birth and resurrection into heaven.

He is holy, and the Apostle Paul encourages us to eat.

The 14th Chapter of Romans basically states that eating something that strengthens our faith in God is good.

But eating something that causes us to stumble or make mistakes is not good; therefore, God should be consulted before eating.

The Bible also says the kingdom of God is not meat and drink, but righteousness, peace, and joy in the Holy Ghost (Romans 14:17).

Jesus said not to worry about food for the body: the birds of the air neither sow, reap, nor gather into barns, but the Lord feeds them (Matthew 6:28).

In other words, we are to focus on what God wants us to do in the spirit of life and he will feed us our daily bread.

Dear Heavenly Father, I praise you for showing me what food is acceptable for my body, but also for Jesus who fills me with heavenly bread that gives me life everlasting. Amen.

Other Bible References: Leviticus 10:8-11; John 6:51; Hebrews 13:9.

And Saul cast the javelin; for he said, I will smite David even to the wall with it. And David avoided out of his presence twice.

1 Samuel 18:11

King Saul considered David an enemy after David killed the giant Goliath in battle and gained fame among the people.

We may have an enemy like Saul, when someone becomes jealous or resentful, but that's a good time for turning to God.

David prayed for the Lord to have vengeance on Saul, "As the Lord liveth, the Lord shall smite him, or his day shall come to die; or he shall descend into battle, and perish" (1 Samuel 26:10).

Saul did perish in battle, and David was spared the guilt of retaliation, because he had given vengeance's place to God.

God will have vengeance on his adversaries (Deuteronomy 32:35).

He is an enemy to enemies (Numbers 23:22-33).

But this protection only comes from being obedient and following his statutes.

Dear Heavenly Father, Please spare me from this enemy's anger and take him away from me. Confront this enemy in righteousness and judgment, as I keep you first in my life. Amen.

And the Pharisees went forth and straightway took counsel with the Herodians against him, how they might destroy him.

Mark 3:6

Jesus became an enemy of the Pharisees when he started healing on the Sabbath Day of rest. Scribes and priests also considered Jesus an enemy, because he was teaching a new doctrine (Luke 19:47). And the Jews sought to slay Jesus for claiming to be the Son of God (John 5:18).

So Jesus had lots of enemies.

We will have enemies for following Jesus, because he was a righteous man who proclaimed truth from God. Many people become offended at truth.

Jesus says to bless your enemies, and pray for them who despitefully use you (Matthew 5:43-44). Jesus knew that God entreats us favorably when we pray good things for other people.

As a person believes, so be it unto him.

Giving an enemy over to God in prayer allows us to go and complete the work God has for us.

Dear Heavenly Father, I thank you for intercession here to help me be at peace. May my enemy come to know your peace also through the precious blood of Jesus, who died for our sins. Amen.

Other Bible References: Exodus 23:4; Job 31:29; Psalms 68:1, 92 9; Proverbs 25:21; 1 Corinthians 15:25-26; Revelation 21:8.

Evil – Old Testament

But it shall to come to pass, if thou wilt not hearken unto the voice of the Lord thy God, to observe to do all his commandments and his statutes which I command thee this day, that all these curses shall come upon thee, and overtake thee.

Deuteronomy 28:15

God threatens man with evil upon disobedience to his righteous commandments (Genesis 2: 9; Deuteronomy 28: 15-68).

The traits of evil are something we do not want. They are cursing, destruction, pestilence, fever, burning, madness, and slavery.

Fortunately, God has power over all these evils. We only need get right with God to be spared of them.

The fear of the Lord is to hate evil (Proverbs 8:13), and we are advised to depart from evil and do good (Psalm 37:27, Proverbs 3:7).

Innumerable evils encompassed a psalmist -- iniquities consumed and shamed him -- but he made the Lord his trust for mercy and salvation (Psalm 40).

Dear Lord, Thank you for having control over evil. Your righteousness will prevail in this situation and I trust you to keep me safe. Amen.

Evil – New Testament

Let him eschew evil, and do good, let him seek peace, and ensue it.

1 Peter 3:11

Before we can eschew evil, we must define it.

Adjectives for evil in the New Testament are slander, pride, deceit, maliciousness, backbiting, hatred, drunkenness, jealousy, malignity, covetousness, lust, self-willingness, idolatry, witchcraft, reveling, debate, false accusation, fierceness, and murder.

Meddling with any of those traits is meddling with evil.

Jesus says evil comes from within the heart of man (Mark 7:21-23).

Demon possessed people would lose control of their bodies and endanger themselves, but Christ says this kind comes out by prayer and fasting (Matthew 17:14-21).

The hungered Christ conquered the evil lust of the flesh when he refused Satan's offer to turn stones into bread (Matthew 4:3). He conquered the lust for worldly power when he denied Satan's offer to rule the nations (Matthew 4:8-10).And he conquered evil doctrine because he was a righteous man who knew no sin (1 Peter 2:21-22 and 1 John 3:4-6).

Dear Lord, I thank you for Jesus Christ who overcomes evil. And I invite him into my heart for protection, wisdom, and salvation. Amen.

Other Bible References about Evil: Genesis 2:9; Joshua 24:1; Psalms 32:13-16, 34:21, 37:27; Proverbs 16:17, 28:1; Isaiah 45:7; Joel 2:12-13; Matthew 5:39; Mark 7:21-23; Romans 12:9; Righteousness overcomes evil, Psalms 119.

And Joshua blessed him, and gave unto Caleb, the son of Jephunneh, Hebron, for an inheritance.
Joshua 14:13

Caleb faithfully inherited the land he had spied out years earlier but it was not without difficulty: he was slandered and threatened with stoning upon reporting the land and its inhabitants could be overcome.

We will also have troubles before receiving God's promises, but if God has ordained something, it will come true: God is not a man that he should lie (Numbers 23:19).

The Bible also says God's faithfulness does not fail (Psalms 89:33).

Consider reading more of God's attributes of faithfulness in the 89th Chapter of Psalms.

We are to give God the glory in all that we do, and being faithful begins the journey.

Dear Lord, May I obtain the wonderful promises you have for me by faith. Amen.

Faith – New Testament

Now faith is the substance of things hoped for, the evidence of things not seen. For by it, the elders received a good report.

Hebrews 11:1

Faith is something we see in the future, and with God's help, we can obtain its promise.

The devil has tried to disturb such faith, with projection of false images, sounds, and deceivers.

But God is holy.

The practitioners of faith in God are listed in the 11th chapter of Hebrews: they obtained victories in battle, established righteous decrees, and built altars.

But the greatest faith we can have is to believe in the risen Christ who gives salvation from sin. He takes away sin by his death on the cross, and he arose into heaven to give us a new life.

The Bible says, But as many as received him, to them gave he power to become sons of God, even to them that believe on his name (John 1:12).

Christ incorporated faith works of God into his life: he healed people, taught them God's word, and fellowshipped with the lost.

We should be so faithful.

Dear Lord, Let me be faithful to complete the task you have shown me for life, but more so, may I know Jesus as my Savior. Amen.

Other Bible References: Psalms 99, 105, 119:89-91; John 1:12-13; Hebrews 12:1-2.

And Moses and Aaron went and gathered together all the elders of the children of Israel. And Aaron spoke all the words which the Lord had spoken unto Moses, and did the signs of the sight of the people.

Exodus 4:29-30

Fellowshipping with other believers makes great things happen, such as when Moses, Aaron, and the elders of Israel got together and made a plan to free their people from slavery.

As they worshipped God in that meeting, we should worship and acknowledge God in daily activities.

But first, fellowship with God when alone.

When Moses was tending a flock near a mountain, God appeared to him out of a burning bush and made a covenant.

God has said, "I will be sanctified in them that come nigh me, and before all the people I will be glorified" (Leviticus 10:3).

Dear Father in Heaven, I praise you for brothers and sisters who have gifts of your spirit, but also for every human -- that they might find you. Amen.

And when the scribes and Pharisees saw him eat with tax collectors and sinners, they said unto his disciples, "How is it that he eateth and drinketh with tax collectors and sinners?"

Mark 2:16

Jesus sets a wonderful example of fellowshipping with people when he sat down to eat with publicans, sinners, and the sick.

He knew they needed to be fed God's word, so he humbled himself before them.

We should be so humble -- in front of people with different faiths and experiences.

Not only can we share our lives, but give testimony of our faith in God. We might find that we have something in common.

Remember, we were once strangers to God (Ephesians 2:19), but God had mercy to fellowship with us.

The Bible also encourages us to fellowship in the congregation of believers: "Not forsaking the assembly of ourselves together, as the manner of some is; but exhorting one another: and so much the more, as ye see the day approaching" (Hebrews. 10:25).

Dear Lord, I thank you for my brothers and sisters all over the world. May we unite to proclaim the good news of salvation to all people. Amen.

Other Bible References: Psalms 58:3, 133:1; Proverbs 4:14, 12:11, 14:7; Luke 5:32, 6:32-34; Philippians 2:1-2; Ephesians 5:11.

And Joseph said unto them, "Fear not; for am I in the place of God?"

Genesis 50:6

Only a holy God can redeem sin but Joseph's brothers wanted Joseph to forgive them for abandoning him years earlier.

God says, "I, even I, am He who blotteth out thy transgressions for mine own sake, and will not remember sins" (Isaiah 43:25). The Bible further confirms that forgiveness is with God (Psalms 130:4).

Consider reading King David's path to forgiveness in Psalms 51, after he sinned with Bathsheba.

He asked for mercy, acknowledged sin, and committed himself to teach other people about God's ways.

The words given to David's son Solomon may sum up the path to finding forgiveness. "If my people, who are called by my name, shall humble themselves, and pray, and seek my face, and turn from their wicked ways, then will I hear from heaven, and will forgive their sin, and will heal their land" (2 Chronicles 7:14).

Dear Lord, I humbly confess my sin. Please forgive me and create a new heart within me to serve you in righteousness. Amen

Forgiveness – New Testament

"And when ye stand praying, forgive, if ye have ought against any, that your Father also, who is in heaven, may forgive you your trespasses."

Mark 11:25

Jesus says the first requirement to being personally forgiven by God of sin is to forgive all other people of sin.

However, we may have sinned against God himself by failing to put him first in tithing, activities, and family loyalty.

For these sins to be removed, they must be completely acknowledged and put on the back on God's Son, Jesus, who takes away sin.

Christ Jesus is the pure sacrifice for our sins that allows us to become completely forgiven.

The Bible says, If we confess our sins, he is faithful and just to forgive us our sins, and to cleanse us from all unrighteousness (1 John 1: 9-2:2).

Sins may take years to redeem, but we are encouraged to patiently redeem the time (Ephesians 5:9-17).

Dear Lord, I confess my sins and abandon them. And I thank you for Christ who took my sins upon His back to the cross. Forgiveness is truly with you, and your mercy endures forever. Amen.

Other Bible References: Psalms 25:16-18, 86:5-8, 130:1-4; Romans 9:15-18; Ephesians 1:3-14, 4:32.

Friends – Old Testament

Now when Job's three friends heard of all this evil that was come upon him, they came everyone from his own place; Eliphaz the Tenamite, and Bildad the Shuhite, and Zophar the Naamathite: for they had made an appointment together to come to mourn with him and to comfort him.
Job 2:11

Friends came to Job's side after he suffered loss of family, farm, and health, but none could comfort him, and Job said, "Miserable comforters are ye all."

Friends do not always understand our problems.

Consider getting to know God as a friend, so when difficult times come, you will have someone to trust.

For domestic friendship, the Bible says, To have friends, one must show himself friendly (Proverbs 18:24), and a friend loves at all times (Proverbs 17:17).

Nevertheless, we are advised never to completely trust a friend (Micah 7:5); but in contrast, there is a friend who [stays] closer than a brother (Proverbs 18:24).

Dear Father in Heaven, Thank you for friends, but you are my true friend and I humbly seek your face for eternal companionship. Amen.

If there be therefore any consolation in Christ, if any comfort of love, if any fellowship of the Spirit, if any bowels and mercies, Fulfill ye my joy, that ye be like-minded, having the same love, being of one accord, of one mind. Let nothing be done through strife or vainglory; but in lowliness of mind let each esteem other better than themselves.
Philippians 2:1-3

Performing all those precepts makes many friends, but we should also consider Jesus as a friend.

He said, "Henceforth, I call you not servants; for the servant knoweth not what his lord doeth: but I have called you friends; for all things that I have heard of my Father I have made known unto you" (John 15:15).

Jesus shares with us the wonderful truth from God about finding salvation.

May we think about opening our hearts to let Jesus in and be our friend. He has given the ultimate sacrifice for us by laying down his life.

Dear Lord, I humble myself before my friends to listen, encourage, and help, but may Jesus Christ be our true bond for friendship that keeps us joyful in God's Holy Spirit.

Other Bible References: Proverbs 16:28, 27:6; John 15:12 .

And Samson said unto them, "I will now put forth a riddle unto you: if ye can certainly declare it me within the seven days of the feast, and find it out, then I will give you thirty sheets and thirty change of garments."

Judges 14:12

Samson gambled that his friends couldn't solve a riddle about a honeycomb being in a lion's carcass, and he lost.

Then he gambled his new wife Delilah couldn't find the source of his strength, and he lost again when a man shaved the locks of Samson's hair to weaken him.

Samson's final gamble came when he pulled down the pillars of an outdoor stadium, and he lost his life, though he had asked God for permission to avenge his enemies.

Possibly, we are on the losing end of a gambling spree, but want to save our life.

The only way we can do so is commit our ways and assets to God.

God already owns all, but he expects us to return a portion of assets to him (Genesis 28:22; Leviticus 27:30-34).

And he always wants our time and service.

Dear Lord, Thank you for providing me assets. May I invest them for your purpose rather than mine, and be in the right place to serve you. Amen.

Gambling – New Testament

And when he had spent all, there arose a mighty famine in that land, and he began to be in want.
Luke 15: 14

Jesus tells a story about a young man going out and wasting his father's goods with riotous living and becoming famished; then the boy wanted to return home.

His father was waiting for him with open arms.

Our Father in heaven welcomes us when we acknowledge wasting assets and time. He has had mercy upon thousands of people who love him.

The wisest investment we can make is giving our life to God. We will be in the right place to receive a sure return on our investment.

The peace of mind that comes from being with God is a reward that is free upon our confession of sin.

Dear Lord, Thank you for providing Christ who has died for my sin. I confess my sin and promise to commit all my assets to you. Sustain me with your provisions I pray. Amen.

Other Bible References: Matthew 25:14-30; Luke 16:1-31; 19:19-26; Timothy 6:18.

Humble – Old Testament

And thou shalt remember all the way the Lord thy God led thee this forty years in the wilderness, to humble, and to prove thee, to know what was in thine heart, whether thou wouldest keep his commandments or not.
Deuteronomy 8:2

God often humbles us in life to know he is God, as he did the Israelites in the wilderness, when they had no food, water, or home.

Either we submit to His authority, or we continue in prideful ways to destruction.

Moses scorned the people for their stubbornness and disobedience (Deuteronomy 9).

Consider beginning each day humbly in prayer to God, for the Bible says, Humility is life (Proverbs 22:4).

The writer of Psalms 69 was humbled: poor, sorrowful, reproached by enemies, drowning in waters, hated, ashamed, and with no friends; yet he praised God with a song and gave thanks (Psalms 69:30).

The humble shall see this and be glad; and your heart shall live that seek God (Palms 69:32).

Dear Lord, My heart is not haughty, nor mine eyes lofty: neither do I exercise myself in great matters, or in things too high for me. Surely I have behaved and quieted myself, as a child that is weaned of his mother: my soul is even as a weaned child; (Psalms 131). Amen.

Humble – New Testament

Whosoever, therefore, shall humble himself as the little child, the same is greatest in the kingdom of heaven.
Matthew 18:4

Being humble lowers one self.

Pride is abandoned, selfish desires are gone, and there is a willingness to serve God and man.

Humility also receives spiritual correction.

The Bible says this correction allows us to partake of God's holiness and yields the peaceable fruits of righteousness (Hebrews 12:8-11).

If you have a problem being humble, consider fasting from food periodically to know God alone can meet your needs. Consider listening more than speaking.

Jesus quietly listened to problems and humbled himself before man and God.

Humility is a virtue that protects us, for the Bible says that God gives grace to the humble (1 Peter 5:5).

Dear God, Humble me to be more like Jesus, who served the people's needs and was obedient to you. Amen.

Other Bible References: Matthew 5:5, 18:3; Luke 14:11; Philippians 2:8; Hebrews 12:2.

And Joseph's master took him and put him into the prison, a place where the king's prisoners were bound: and he was there in the prison.

Genesis 39:20

Joseph was falsely accused by his master's wife of seduction and put into prison.

But when the ruler Pharaoh wanted a dream interpreted, he called for the righteous man Joseph and freed him.

Joseph had kept his faith in God for freedom, though in prison.

Imprisonment is a terrible, lonely experience: the rooms are dark, the conditions are controlled, and people cannot be trusted, but God is still there for anyone who calls on His name.

Psalms 145 and 146 inspires a prisoner to hope in the living God.

The Lord upholdeth all that fall, and raiseth up all those who are bowed down (Psalms 145:14). And he has the power to free the prisoners (Psalms 146:7).

Dear Father in Heaven, This jail is dreadful, yet I know you have the power to give me freedom. I call upon your name in truth, mercy, and faith to protect and have mercy on me. Amen.

"Are they ministers of Christ? (I speak as a fool.) I am more: in labors more abundant, in stripes above measure, in prisons more frequently, in deaths often."
2 Corinthians 11:23

The Apostle Paul was a prisoner for Christ's sake, but many of us are prisoners because we disobeyed the law.

However, the law is our schoolmaster that brings us to know Christ (Galatians 3:24).

Christ Jesus has passed through this veil of darkness to give us access to God and light upon confession of sin (Hebrews 6: 18:19). Acceptance of Christ turns our lives around.

Christ said he came "to preach deliverance to the captives and set at liberty those who are bruised" (Luke 4:18).

Experiencing this new birth and freedom in Christ makes us want share the story.

The Apostle Paul shared the gospel of salvation with a keeper of the prison, and he became saved from death (Acts 16:19).

Dear Father in Heaven, I thank you for your wonderful word of life. You give me hope in Christ – being a friend I can trust. Protect me I pray. Amen.

Other Bible References: Luke 23:43; John 8:36; Romans 8:2; Galatians 3:25, 5:1; Philippians 2:8.

Jealousy – Old Testament

And Saul eyed David, from that day and forward.
1 Samuel 18:9

Saul became jealous after David killed a giant named Goliath and became a hero among the people. David was also good looking and loved by his family.

But if we know God, we should not become jealous of anyone or anything: it is God whom we love first in obedience to His First Commandment: Thou shalt have no other gods before me (Exodus 20:3).

But God does have a right to be jealous. He becomes jealous when we worship anything or anyone other than him (Deuteronomy 32:21); and he will correct us to know he is God.

We don't want to become the objects of someone's vengeance prayer -- but want to draw close to God in devotion and love.

Dear Lord, I abandon jealousy to worship and put you first in my life. I am content to serve you in righteousness, mercy, and truth. Amen.

Let us not be desirous of vain glory, provoking one another, envying one another.
Galatians 5:26

Our focus should be on God's Son Jesus rather than another person -- conforming more to the image of this heavenly Savior who is able to intercede and save us (Romans 8:29; 12:1-16).

The Bible says, If ye then be risen with Christ, seek those things which are above, where Christ sitteth on the right hand of God. Set your affection on things above, not on things on the earth (Colossians 3:1-2).

Consider Christ -- who took on himself no reputation, worldly title, expensive clothes, or personal assets - but was received by God as a Son.

Each of us who confesses Christ is received by God to have a unique gift of the spirit (1 Corinthians 12:11).

Dear Lord, Humble me so that I am not envious of anyone or anything. You are my life, and I thank you for my friends in Christ Jesus. Amen.

Other Bible References about Jealousy: Proverbs 3:31, 6:34, 14: 30, 23:17, 27:4; 1 Corinthians 13:4; Romans 13:13; James 3:17-18, 4:5-6.

And he will love thee, and bless thee, and multiply thee;
he will also bless the fruit of thy womb, and the fruit of thy
land . . . .

Deuteronomy 7:13

Happiness may be defined as the freedom to do as we
please, but with God in the Old Testament, happiness is
defined as obeying His laws and loving him with all thine
heart, mind, soul, and strength (Deuteronomy 6-8; 28:1-14).

But there will be troubles to pursuing happiness:
sickness, enemies, sin, or hunger will take place.

Consider acknowledging God in your life and following
His plan for happiness.

Our plans are doomed to fail, but God's plan always
works despite the hardships.

Dear Lord, I thank you for being here. Your joy is truly
my strength. I confess my sins and free my mind to work
and glorify you. Amen.

Joyfulness – New Testament

And the angel said unto them, "Fear not: for, behold, I bring you good tidings of great joy, which shall be to all people."

Luke 2:10

The shepherds became joyful when they heard the good news of Christ's birth, so they immediately went to Bethlehem to see the child.

Upon seeing the Savior, they returned home praising and glorifying God.

The righteous man, Simeon, who had waited long for the consolation of Israel, was also joyful, as he held the baby in his arms and blessed God.

And Christ's mother, Mary, said a lengthy prayer that praised God.

Christ is a risen Savior who frees us from sin and allows us to enter the joy of our Father in heaven. He was born for our salvation, and it gives us happiness to know him.

Dear Father in Heaven, It was for joy Jesus was born to take away sin. Thank you for releasing me of sin to have pure joy on earth. Amen.

Other Bible References: Ecclesiastes 2:24; Job 41:22; Psalms 16:11, 51:12; Proverbs 14:10; Lamentations 2:15; Luke 15:7; John 3:29; Philippians 2:12; 1 Peter 1:8.

Loneliness –Old Testament

And the Lord God said, "It is not good that the man should be alone: I will make him a help meet [proper] for him."

Genesis 2:18

Loneliness is one reason why God created a woman -- to be with the man.

However, some people are called to be separate, such as a Nazarene, who vowed a vow of separation (Numbers 6). Also, a eunuch was encouraged to not think they he was a dry tree, but the Lord says they have a place within his walls and house (Isaiah 56:3-5).

During a feeling of loneliness, make sure your relationship with God is intact (Read Psalm 81). God has promised to be with us if we love and obey him.

Also, consider fellowshipping with other believers.

The Bible says, Bless ye God in the congregations, even the Lord, from the fountain of Israel (Psalms 68:26).

Dear Lord, This loneliness is a good time to learn more about You. I praise You for being here, and I thank You for other believers who worship in the world. Amen.

Loneliness – New Testament

. . . I will never leave thee, nor forsake thee.
Hebrews 13:5

The 13th Chapter of Hebrews affirms that God is with us, so we should never think of being alone.

But if we don't know God, we are indeed alone: we are like the branches without a vine as Jesus described in John 15:1-6.

Confessing Jesus, who is like a vine that provides the path to God (John 14:23); we become *one* with the Lord. And the Holy Spirit resides with us (John 15:26).

Jesus treasured his time alone with his Father in Heaven. He would go to the desert, mountain caves, and gardens to spend time in private prayer.

Praising and pleasing God helps us know that we are not alone.

However, we are to fellowship, encourage one another, entertain strangers, and worship in the congregation.

Dear Lord, I praise you here in my loneliness, and I thank you for Jesus who died for my sin. May my loneliness be turned into joy with the Holy Spirit and others who praise your holy name. Amen.

Other Bible References about Loneliness: Joshua 1:9; Psalms 18:6, 68:5-6, 133:1; Matthew 5:16; Romans 10:13, 20; I John 1:3.

Lost – Old Testament

Now for a long season, Israel hath been without the true God, and without a teaching priest, and without law.
2 Chronicles 15:3

The people of Israel were spiritually lost: there was no peace in the land, nation destroyed nation, city destroyed city, and great vexations occurred.

So God sent Azania the prophet to meet Asa, King of Israel, and said, "The Lord is with you while you are with him; and if ye seek him, he will be found by you . . ." (v. 2).

Establishing a covenant with God begins a journey to become found and have peace.

King Asa put away all the golden images and abominable idols that were defiling the land and people; he renewed the altar of the Lord.

The people returned to obey the law of God with all their heart and soul.

The Bible says, Blessed is the man that walketh not in the counsel of the ungodly, nor standeth in the way of sinners, nor sitteth in the seat of the scornful. But his delight is in the law of the Lord . . . he shall be like a tree planted by the rivers of water . . . (Psalms 1:1).

This tree remains in a place of nourishment, as we who become found by the word of God.

Dear Lord, I praise you for being here in my stillness. You are my home by belief and faith. Grant me peace, rest, and happiness. Amen.

Lost -- New Testament

For the Son of Man is come to save that which was lost.
Matthew 18:11

Jesus is able to save the lost because he can remove sins.

The Bible says many people have fallen victim to false doctrine and are led astray -- that some shall depart from the faith, giving heed to seducing spirits, and doctrines of devils (1 Timothy 4:1).

When you feel lost, consider humbling yourself and seeking God with your whole heart.

God is an anchor for the soul (Hebrews 6:19).

And Christ commands us to love the Lord thy God with all thy heart, and with all thy soul, and with all thy mind, and with all thy strength – and thy neighbor as thyself (Mark 12:30-31).

Also, obeying Christ's sermon on the mount, keeps us in the right attitude: "Blessed are the poor in spirit: for theirs is the kingdom of heaven . . ." (Matthew 5:1-12).

Dear Lord, Life is so confusing, but I trust you to lead me safely and righteously. May I have peace, rest, and happiness. Amen.

Other Bible References: Psalms 119:176; Proverbs 4:20-27; Isaiah 48:17, 55:6; Matthew 10:39; Romans 10:20; Ephesians 4:14-15.

"Where thou diest, will I die, and there will I be buried; the Lord do so to me, and more also if anything but death part thee and me."

Ruth 1:17

Ruth gives us a wonderful example of love when she vows to stay by her mother-in-law's side until death.

Naomi's two sons had died, and she wanted to make a treacherous trip to her homeland.

Our love for each other should be so strong, but our first love should be for God.

God commands us: And thou shalt love the Lord thy God with all thine heart, and with all thy soul, and with all thy might (Deuteronomy 6:5).

Expressing God's love for others; however, testifies of our faith and concurs with God's word: Thou shalt not avenge, nor bear any grudge against the children of thy people, but thou shalt love thy neighbor as thyself: I am the Lord (Leviticus 19:18).

Ruth returned with Naomi to her homeland and was rewarded with rest and safety.

Dear Lord, I love you with all my heart, mind, soul, and strength. May I set an example of love towards others with humble service that glorifies You and produces good work in mercy. Amen.

Love – New Testament

Charity suffereth long, and is kind; charity envieth not; charity vaunteth not itself, is not puffed up . . . .
1 Corinthians 13:4-8

Before we can express love, we need to define its sixteen characteristics in the scriptures.

Love is patient. Love is kind. Love is not envious. Love is not vain. Love is not puffed up. Love does not behave itself indecently. Love does not pursue its own things. Love is not easily provoked. Love thinks no evil. Love does not rejoice over wrong. Love rejoices with the truth. Love quietly covers all things. Love believes all things. Love hopes all things. Love endures all things. Love never fails.

Quietly think about each item and how to apply it towards other people.

But Christ has expressed the greatest love when he gave up his life for our sins (John 15:13).

After accepting Christ into our lives, we are free to serve the living God and share the news with other people.

Christ summarizes the attitude we should have towards others when he said, "that ye love one another, as I have loved you" (John 15:12).

Dear God, I praise you for Jesus, who provides me the path to love you more. Amen.

Other Bible References: Deuteronomy 6:5; Proverbs 8:17, 15:9; Hosea 14:4; John 3:16, 13:34, 14:21, 15:13; Romans 5:8; 1 John 4:7, 16-19.

And Jacob said unto his father, "I am Esau, thy first-born; I have done according to thou badest me: arise, I pray thee, sit and eat of my venison, that thy soul may bless me."
Genesis 27:19

Jacob lied to his nearly blind father about being Esau so he would get his older brother's blessing.

We may lie to get something we want, or try to be something we aren't, but God will confront our lies at some time in life because he loves us enough to correct us.

Years later, God's messenger confronted Jacob in a private place, where an angel wrestled Jacob to the ground and taught him a lesson about who was in charge.

God forbid it takes an injury before we face the truth, but usually something bad happens before we admit truth (read more about God confronting lies: Psalms 50:16-23; 90:8).

The Bible says, Thou shalt not bear false witness against thy neighbor (Exodus 20:16); and thou shalt not raise a false report (Exodus 23:1).

Dear Lord, Forgive me for lying, and have mercy on me. May I tell the truth from now on. May my apology be accepted. Amen.

Lying – New Testament

But Peter said, "Ananias, why hath Satan filled thine heart to lie to the Holy Ghost, and to keep back part of the price of the land?"   *Acts 5:3*

The Apostles had agreed to put all their assets in a common treasury and share alike, but Ananias and his wife kept back part of their holdings.

Ananias must have thought he had gotten away with his secret plan to keep some of his money, but Peter confronted him about it. And when Ananias was confronted by the Holy Spirit, he was struck dead (Acts 5:1-5).

Rather than face God's harsh judgment, we should come to the truth right now: we cannot always trust ourselves. We are sinners who need Christ Jesus to face real facts (Ephesians 4:21-29).

It is the devil who is a liar, as Christ described: he was a murderer from the beginning, and abode not in the truth; when he speaketh a lie, he speaketh of his own; for he is a liar, and the father of it (John 8:44).

The Bible says, Wherefore, putting away lying, speak every man truth with his neighbor; for we are members one of another (Ephesians 4:25).

Consider also reading Colossians 3:5-17 for living a life of truth.

Dear Father in Heaven, Forgive me for lying, and help me confess the truth. I praise You for Jesus who died for my sin to let me live in truth. Amen.

Other Bible References: Exodus 23:1; Numbers 23:19; Psalms 15:1-3, 31:18, 51:6, 119:163, 145:18; Proverbs 12:19, 21:23; Isaiah 63:8; Zechariah 8:16; Matthew 12:18, 36; John 3:32; Ephesians 2:4; Hebrews 6:18; 1 Peter 3:10; I John 1:8-10, 2:22-29; Revelation 21:8; Psalm 120, Deliverance from lying lips.

And Abraham said unto his eldest servant of his house that ruled over all that he had, "Put, I pray thee, thy hand under my thigh; and I will make thee swear by the Lord, the God of heavens, and the God of all the earth, that thou shalt not take a wife unto my son of the daughters of the Canaanites, among whom I dwell."

Genesis 24:2-3

Abraham certainly wanted no more of the Canaanites, praying that his son would find a wife from the homeland.

Finding a mate among God's people eliminates a lot of problems, because there is an agreement that God is the first priority for life.

When the servant arrived in God's land, he sat by a well of water waiting for a kind woman to come and draw water.

Rebekah came, and offered water to the servant and his animals.

The servant took this as a sign from God that the kind woman Rebekah would be a bride for Isaac.

As men, we might look among God's people for a kind woman to marry.

And women might be kind to strangers, who know the Lord and speak from their heart.

But the most important thing is agreement in God.

Rebekah, and her future husband Isaac, both spoke of God, and were rewarded with children and wealth.

Dear Lord, I look to you for the right mate, but first, I want to make sure my own spiritual house is in order. Forgive my sin and bring me into a right relationship with You. Amen.

Wives, submit, yourselves unto your own husbands, as unto the Lord. For the husband is the head of the wife, even as Christ is the head of the church: and he is the savior of the body . . . Husbands, love your wives, even as Christ also loved the church, and gave himself for it.
Ephesians 5:22-25

Christ is the true bond for marriage because he takes away sin, intercedes in prayer, and provides a path to oneness in God.

When there is a disagreement, look to Christ for agreement. Where there is fault, forgive one another, as God in his abundant mercy has forgiven us (Ephesians 4:32).

Finally, be ye all of one mind, having compassion one of another; love as brethren, be pitiful, be courteous (1 Peter 3:8). (Consider reading the full text of Peter's advice for married couples in 1 Peter 3:1-12.)

Marriage is honorable in all, and the bed becomes undefiled (Hebrews 13:4).

Dear Lord, I praise you for this marriage. May our lives be of grace, peace, righteousness, love, mercy, and happiness in Jesus. Amen.

Other Bible References about Marriage: Genesis 1:17, 2:18; Matthew 19:4-6; Ephesians 5:22-33; Colossians 3:18-19; Redemptive laws for husband and wife, Numbers 30.

Mercy – Old Testament

The Lord is merciful and gracious, slow to anger, and plenteous in mercy.

Psalms 103:8

There are ten traits of God's mercy in Psalms 103.

The Lord forgives sins, heals diseases, redeems life from destruction, covers with love and tenderness, and puts good words in our mouths. Our youth is renewed. There is righteousness and judgment for the oppressed. Mercy is higher than the heavens; sin is removed forever; and mercy is everlasting.

How wonderful it is to know we can enjoy all these mercies!

But they are dependent on a few items: reverential fear of God (verse 17), keeping His covenant, and performing His commandments (verse 18).

God's mercy endures forever for those people who love him.

Dear Father in Heaven, Thank you for providing these mercies for all of us. May each of us depend on your word for life, and obey your commandments. Amen.

Mercy – New Testament

"Blessed are the merciful, for they shall obtain mercy."
Matthew 5:7

Jesus teaches us that if we show mercy to others, we will receive mercy.

Christ gives a good illustration of mercy when he shared a story about a stranger who had fallen among thieves and was beaten (Luke 10:30-37).

A good Samaritan bound up the man's wounds, housed him, and gave him some money.

We should be performing such acts: acquiring something for someone in need, nursing the sick, or donating to the poor.

Remember, God was merciful to us as sinners to provide Jesus as a sacrifice for our sins (Hebrews 10:28).

The least we can do is show God's love for people with humble service.

Dear Father in Heaven, I thank you for Jesus who took my sins to the cross to give me rest. May I tell others about this mercy and show them mercy, as you have shown me. Amen.

Other Bible References about Mercy: 2 Chronicles 7:14; Psalms 25:16-18, 116:1-7; Proverbs 3:3, 21:21, 28:13; Micah 6:8; Matthew 5:7; Luke 6:36; Ephesians 2:4-5; Hebrews 12:11.

And if thy way be too long for thee, so that thou art not able to carry it . . . then shalt thou turn it into money, and bind up the money in thine hand, and shalt go unto the place which the Lord thy God shall choose.
Deuteronomy 14:24-25

Money is a component God incorporated to lessen our load, not make it heavier.

If we have some extra, we should increase tithes to the Lord, invest in the market (for his glory), or distribute liberally to the poor.

What we are not to do is hoard money, for the Bible says, There is a sore evil which I have seen under the sun, namely, riches kept for the owners thereof to their hurt. But those riches perish by evil travail . . . (Ecclesiastes 5:13-14).

Our desire should be as King Solomon, who did not ask God for riches or wealth, but asked God for wisdom and understanding.

And God blessed him with material wealth (2 Chronicles 1: 11-12).

Dear Lord, I put you first in my life, and I trust you to supply my needs. May my assets be invested to extend your kingdom. Amen.

. . . Ye cannot serve God and [money].
                                    Matthew 6:24

Serving God focuses on spiritual things, and not seeking worldly wealth.

Peace, happiness, rest, and humility are some traits that benefit us.

Jesus says all other things, (such as needful provisions to live), shall be added (Matthew 6:26-33).

A rich man had trouble understanding the precept of living a long life.

Jesus told him to sell what he had, distribute to the poor, and follow him (Luke 18:18-22).

Jesus illustrates this teaching by earlier saying: lay not up treasures on earth but in heaven, where moth nor rust corrupts, and thieves cannot steal: for where our treasure is, there will our heart be also (Matthew 6:19-21).

Consider beginning each day with a prayer that wants to serve God.

He is a rewarder to those that believe in him (Hebrews 11:6).

Dear Father in Heaven, You are my first desire, and I commit my way to you. Thank you for providing my riches in Christ Jesus and my daily bread. Amen.

Other Bible References about Money: Psalms 49:6-20; Proverbs 3:9-10, 28-20, 30:8-9; Isaiah 55:1; Mark 10:23-25, 12:4; Luke 12:33-34, 18:22, 19:23; Philippians 4:19: 1 Timothy 6:10-18; James 5:1-6.

Now the word of the Lord came unto Jonah, the son of Amittai, saying, "Arise, go to Nineveh, that great city, and cry against it: for their wickedness is come up before me," but Jonah rose up to flee unto Tarshish from the presence of the Lord.

Jonah 1:1-3

Jonah knew where he was supposed to go and what he was supposed to do, but he went the opposite way.

That's what we do sometimes: the Lord wants us to go somewhere and do something, but we go the opposite way.

Jonah found himself in the middle of a big storm on a sinking boat with an angry crew for disobeying God's command to go and preach to the city of Nineveh. The crew then decided to get rid of him by sending him into the water.

The Bible says obedience is better than sacrifice (1 Samuel 15:22).

Though God loves whom He corrects, we do not want to be cast overboard like Jonah, who was swallowed up by a whale and spit upon on a beach.

Dear Lord, It is difficult to obey, but I choose to be humble and obedient. Bless me Lord as I faithfully endure Your word for life. Amen.

And being found in fashion as a man, he humbled himself and became obedient, unto death, even the death of the cross.

Philippians 2:8

God's son Christ sets a wonderful example of obedience when he received a command to die for the people's sins and walked to a court of judgment to be sentenced to death and hung on a tree post.

Though our purpose is to live and proclaim the good news of the sacrificial death of Christ, we should do so without complaining – knowing God has reserved something better in heaven for us as believers (Hebrews 12:2).

The Apostles affirmed that God is the ultimate rewarder in life, and they submitted to God's will rather than man's (Acts 5:9). Our final accountability is to God (Romans 14:11-12).

Nevertheless, we are to obey those who have the rule over us (Hebrews 13:17), that we might also obtain a good report.

Dear Father in Heaven, Christ's obedience inspires me to follow your calling and do it with joy, knowing that I too will be delivered into something better. May I fulfill the mission of presenting Christ as Savior to the world. Amen.

Other Bible References: Exodus 19:5, 24:7; Deuteronomy 4—8; 2 Corinthians 2:9.

Patience – Old Testament

And Jacob served seven years for Rachel: and they seemed unto him but a few days, for the love he had to her.
Genesis 29:20

Jacob waited fourteen years for Rachel because Uncle Laban deceitfully had given him Leah seven years earlier.

Jacob had lots of patience waiting for the one he loved, but he didn't sit idle: he multiplied cattle to become rich.

While being patient for one thing to happen that God has ordained, we can get busy on something else that gives God glory.

We are encouraged to be patient. "My soul, wait thou upon God; for my expectation is from Him," the psalmist says (Psalm 62:5).

We are to trust God for all things (Psalms 37).

What we are not to do is hasten after and serve another god, while waiting for the promise (Psalms 16:4).

Dear Lord, Your patience is infinite and your understanding forever. While I wait for your promise of eternal joy, I will continue to work for your glory. Amen.

Patience – New Testament

For ye have need of patience, that, after ye have done the will of God, ye might receive the promise.
Hebrews 10:36

The promise that we receive one day is being able to rest in heaven from all our works that have been accomplished upon earth (Revelation 14:12-13).

Until that time, we are encouraged to endure suffering and life with patience (James 5:7-18; 1 Peter 2:20).

The Bible further says, Troubles work patience (Romans 5:3); the trying of our faith worketh patience (James 1:3); and we are to let patience have her perfect work (James 1:4).

Jesus was mocked, defamed, and beaten, yet he patiently endured, with his Father in Heaven.

Jesus says, "In your patience, possess ye your souls" (Luke 21:19).

Dear Lord, Your patience is everlasting and I wait upon you to receive the promise. May I be productive for Your sake. Amen.

Other Bible References about Patience: Psalms 23:14, 37:7, 40:1; Proverbs 25:8; Ecclesiastes 7: 8; Matthew 24:13; Luke 8:15, 21:19; James 1:2-4, 5:7-8; 1 Peter 2:20.

And there was a strife between the headsmen of Abram's cattle and the herdsmen of Lot's cattle . . . .
Genesis 13:7

Abraham and Lot's herdsmen were about to fight over grazing land for their animals, so Abram called a meeting, and the two men met at an intersection overlooking a vast amount of land and came to an agreement: Lot would occupy one part of the land while Abraham the other.

But it was Abram who yielded first, letting Lot choose a pasture.

When there is a disagreement with someone, consider yielding to the other person for peace: it may mean God has something better.

Lot had chosen the plain of Jordan, but the men of those cities were wicked, and Lot was taken captive.

If there is no peace in our personal lives, then we should yield to a God who has power over our lives.

Agreement with God brings peace, rather than fighting, arguing, and rebellion.

Dear Lord, I humble myself from fighting and arguing, and I seek the peace that comes from you. The battle is yours Lord. Amen.

Peace – New Testament

Peace I leave with you, my peace I give unto you; not as the world giveth, give I unto you. Let not your heart be troubled, neither let it be afraid.

John 14:27

Jesus is able to give us peace because he takes away sin, provides a path to God, and has gone to heaven to prepare a place for us.

But many of us think peace is at a beach, virgin forest, or a mountain stream. While these places give us physical peace by the absence of sound, emotional peace comes from agreement with God through Jesus Christ (Romans 5:1).

A man, who was cutting himself and had no peace, was found sitting in his right mind after he met Jesus (Mark 5:1-20).

But domestically, Jesus did not come to bring peace, but division -- knowing his new testament would separate the people (Luke 12:51-53).

Yet the Apostle Paul said that Jesus has established peace -- by breaking down the middle wall of partition of different faiths (Ephesians 2:13-16).

Dear Lord, Knowing you gives me peace, and I thank you for Jesus, providing the way to find You. Amen.

Other Bible References about Peace: Leviticus 26:6; Job 34:29-30; Psalms 4:8, 34:14, 119:165; Proverbs 16:7, 17:1; Ecclesiastes 4:6; Isaiah 26:3, 30:5; Matthew 5:9; John 14:27; Philippians 4:7; Colossians 3:15; Hebrews 12:14; 1 Peter 3:11.

And the officers of the children of Israel, whom Pharaoh's task makers had set over them, were beaten . . . .
Exodus 5:14

The officers were beaten because their workers could not keep up with a workload Pharaoh kept increasing.

Pharaoh was trying to hinder the people from worshipping their God.

Persecutors may increase our workload, defame us, or even try to kill us, but God is going to allow His people to worship him.

Eventually, he saved the children of Israel from Pharaoh's pursuing army and gave them a place to build an altar.

Our primary responsibility is to God, and not man.

Though we honor parents and respect brethren, it is God who is ultimately our judge and a rewarder of spiritual blessings. He wants us to witness for him and proclaim His name (Deuteronomy 4:14-20).

Dear Lord, "O Lord my God, in thee do I put my trust; save me from all those who persecute me, and deliver me;" Psalm 7:1. Amen.

Persecution – New Testament

Yea, and all that will live godly in Christ Jesus shall suffer persecution.

2 Timothy 3:12

Living godly in Christ Jesus exposes believers to persecution because they are sanctified. The devil loves nothing more than to want something without having to bow down and confess Christ.

The devil also wants to blame and afflict innocent people rather than accept his own discipline and punishment.

The devout man Stephen, who was accused of subverting the law and slandering Moses, was stoned to death for testifying of Christ (Acts 6:9-7:60).

When persecutions, slander, threatenings, and afflictions come, look to Jesus who sits on the right hand side of God. He suffered such as we, and he is able to intercede for us.

We are encouraged to resist the devil and be steadfast in the faith (1 Peter 5:9). Be strong in the Lord, and in the power of His might (Ephesians 6:10). And we are to be blameless, such as the archangel Michael, who did not accuse Satan, but said, "The Lord rebukes thee" (Jude 1:9).

Prayer of Jesus: "But I say unto you, Love your enemies, bless them that curse you, do good to them that hate you, and pray for them which despitefully use you, and persecute you" (Matthew 5:44).

Other Bible References about Persecution: Psalms 7:1-2, 9:9, 91:3; Proverbs 24:15-16; John 6:15, 16:13; Romans 8:36-37; 1 Corinthians 4:11-13; 2 Corinthians 4:8-11; Philippians 1:28-30; 2 Timothy 3:12; James 5:16; Hebrews 11:37-40; 1 Peter 4:19.

Now when Daniel knew that the writing was signed, he went into his house, and his windows being open in his chamber toward Jerusalem, he kneeled upon his knees three times a day, and prayed and gave thanks before his God, as he did aforetime.

Daniel 6:10

King Darius had signed a decree for all men to come to him when they needed something, but Daniel knew who supplied his needs, and so he prayed towards God's holy temple.

The temple is open to us, but we must humble ourselves to pray as Daniel. (Daniel had also refused the king's food and wine, for he would rather eat vegetables and drink water.)

But consider also the commitment to God by the Biblical man David in Psalms 65:2: O thou who hearest prayer, unto thee shall all flesh come.

David had been through many troubles, but he trusted in God's leadership and direction for life: "Evening, and morning, and at noon, will I pray, and cry aloud, and he shall hear my voice" (Psalms 55:17).

We should be so committed and pray: otherwise, we could be like the chaff the wind blows away (Psalms 1: 4).

But with God, we have purpose, and we know God hears the prayer of the righteous (Proverbs 15:29).

He will not hear a prayer of iniquity (Psalms 66: 18).

Dear Lord, I close my eyes and pour out my emotions to you. Bless me Lord as I listen to Your guidance for my life. Amen.

Prayer -- New Testament

But thou, when thou prayest, enter into thy closet, and when thou hast shut thy door, pray to thy Father, who is in secret; and thy Father, who seeth in secret, shall reward thee openly.

Matthew 6:6

Going into a closed room and being able to commune with almighty God through Jesus Christ is the greatest gift ever given to man.

When troubles come, God is here to fix them. When sickness comes, God is here to heal. When evil comes, God is here with righteousness for victory. And when there's a temptation to sin, God is here with Jesus to help us overcome it.

Divine prayer closes the eyes, addresses God, and listens.

Jesus gives us good examples of intimate prayer with God in the 17th Chapter of John.

Jesus exhorts us saying, "And all things, whatever ye shall ask in prayer, believing, ye shall receive" (Matthew 21:22).

Dear Father in Heaven, I love you and thank you for the sacrifice of Jesus who allows me to commune with you in prayer. Amen.

Other Bible References about Prayer: 2 Chronicles 7:14-15; Psalms 5:1-3, 10:17, 65:1-2, 66:18, 119:164; Proverbs 15:29, 28:9; Isaiah 55:11; Matthew 6:1-13; Mark 1:24; Luke 18:1; Romans 8:26; Ephesians 3:20; 1 Thessalonians 5:17; Philippians 4:6; 1 John 5:14-15; Revelation 3:20.

Pride -- Old Testament

The king spoke, and said, "Is not this great Babylon, that I have built for the house of thy kingdom by the might of my power, and for the honor of my majesty?"
Daniel 4:30

Nebuchadnezzar proudly exclaimed he had built his kingdom by his power, but as he spoke, a voice came from heaven telling him his kingdom would be cut down:

When our pride gets high like Nebuchadnezzar, God will humble us.

The Bible says, Pride goeth before destruction, and a haughty spirit before a fall (Proverbs 16:18).

Nebuchadnezzar was driven to live with the beasts of the fields, but after being humbled, Nebuchadnezzar praised and declared God was just and truthful.

May we acknowledge the rule and glory of God.

"Nor by might, and not by power, but by my spirit, saith the Lord" (Zechariah 4:6).

Dear Lord, Forgive me for being so prideful, and humble me to know you better. Amen.

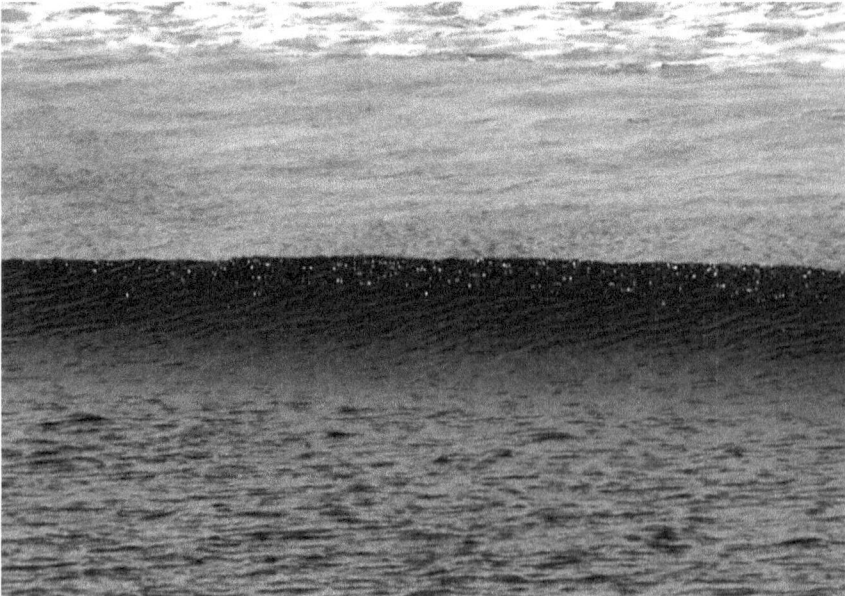

Pride – New Testament

Be of the same mind toward one another. Mind not high things, but condescend to men of low estate. Be not wise in your own conceits.

Romans 3:16

The Bible further says, For all that is in the world, the lust of the flesh, and the lust of the eyes, and the pride of life; is not of the Father, but is of the world. And the world passeth away and the lust of it: but he that doeth the will of God abideth forever (1 John 2:16-17).

Abandoning pride gives us rest.

We do not have to prove anything to anyone, nor strive to be something we aren't. We are simply to trust the Lord and obey His commandments.

The Bible also says, Let nothing be done through strife or vain glory . . . (Philippians 2:3).

The Apostle Paul encourages us to walk worthy of the vocation we are called, with all lowliness and meekness, with long-suffering, forbearing one another in love (Ephesians 4:1-2).

Dear Father in Heaven, I abandon selfish pride to serve you. Amen.

Other Bible References about Pride: Leviticus 26:14-20; Deuteronomy 8:2; Proverbs 11:2, 16:18, 27:2; Psalms 101:5; Habakkuk 2:4; Micah 6:8; Matthew 18:4; Luke 14:11, 18:14; Philippians 2:1-8; 1 Timothy 2:24; James 4:7; 1 Peter 5:6; 1 John 2:16.

"And, behold, I purpose to build a house unto the name of the Lord my God, as the Lord spake unto David my father, saying, 'Thy son, whom I will set upon they throne in thy room, he shall build a house unto my name'."

1 Kings 5:5

One purpose for Solomon was to build a temple where people could worship the Lord; so he hired craftsmen, acquired materials, and had the structure built.

After construction, there was a great feast, and a sermon was preached that glorified God (1 Kings 8:12-66).

Fulfilling God's purpose gives us great joy, because we are pleasing the very God who created us.

But fulfilling a personal purpose will lead to a spiritual void. Consider that King Solomon later strayed from God by having many women concubines.

The Bible says: Blessed is the man whom thou choosest, and causeth to approach unto thee . . . (Psalms 65:4).

May we listen to God's purpose, to give him glory.

Our lives will be complete knowing we are pleasing the living God who made us.

Dear Lord, I thank you for drawing me closer to your purpose for my life. May I experience the joy of serving you. Amen.

Purpose – New Testament

"Ye have not chosen me, but I have chosen you, and ordained you, that ye should go and bring forth fruit, and that your fruit should remain . . . ."

John 15:16

Jesus chose his disciples as God would want, by obedience and a willingness to serve.

The disciples went from town to town speaking of the saving power of Jesus, and they distributed spiritual gifts to needy people.

God still uses believers to produce miracles, heal people, and produce good works. By these administrations of spiritual gifts, God's presence in the world is affirmed, and He gets the glory.

Jesus gives us a good example of fulfilling God's purpose when he said he came to preach the gospel to the poor, heal the brokenhearted, preach deliverance to the captives, the recovering of sight to the blind, and set at liberty them that were bruised (Luke 4:18).

Consider reading Ephesians 1:3-9 to find God's purpose for your life.

Dear Lord, Thank you for showing me the purpose for my life. May I use the spiritual gifts you've given me to heal, teach, and grant mercy to the people of the world. Amen.

Other Bible References: Proverbs 20:18; Isaiah 46:11; Romans 8:28, 9:14-23; Ephesians 3:11, 5:9.

Rejected – Old Testament

The stone which the builders refused is become the head stone of the corner. This is the Lord's doing; it is marvelous in our eyes.

Psalms 118:22

A stone layer will often reject a stone because it does not fit in the straight line of a wall, but when he gets to corner of the wall, it fits.

Life can be like that: we get rejected from some common job yet accepted for something unique, and if know God, out in society proclaiming his word.

Being rejected is a good time to refine talents and increase faith in the Lord.

May we humbly accept the rejection of the world but willingly accept the peace and place of God.

Dear Lord, I have been rejected, but I know you accept me. I humbly bow before you and trust you to guide me to a better place . Amen.

Rejected – New Testament

"The stone the builders rejected is become the head of the corner."

Mark 12:10

Years ago, I had a friend who applied for a job and was immediately rejected; his paper application was filed away.

Despondently leaving the interview, he got in his car to drive home but decided to stop off at the local library to get some books to cheer him up.

Sharing his story with the local parking attendant, he said, "I'm disappointed because I was rejected for a job I really wanted."

The attendant said, "Well, God can take the "d" in disappointment and make it a capital "H" for His appointment."

The man never forgot the words of the parking attendant.

When we are rejected for one thing in the world, God is accepting us for something better.

Dear Father in Heaven, May this disappointment be turned into your appointment. Thank you for eliminating undesirable things from my life. Amen.

Other Bible References about Rejection: 1 Samuel 8:7; Job 42:6-8; Psalms 19:14; Isaiah 41:9, 53:3; Matthews 27:30-31; John 6:37, 12:48-49; 1 Corinthians 1:26-28; Hebrews 10:36, 13:20-21; 1 Peter 2:8.

"I have heard thee by the hearing of the ear, but now my eye seeth thee; wherefore I abhor myself, and repent in dust and ashes."

Job 42:5-6

Job repented from sin only after meeting God face to face.

It takes a meeting with God face to face to be humble and get right.

In Psalms 38:4, King David said iniquities had gone over his head; and he expressed sorrow for his sin.

In Ezra 9-10, the people of Israel had suffered captivity and confusion, because they had disobeyed God's commandments.

God convicted their conscience of sin when he sent Ezra to confront them, and they agreed to change (repent).

They entered a covenant with the Lord that renewed their faith and obedience to the law.

When iniquities have gone over our heads, and sorrow occurs, it's time to repent and get right with God.

We are encouraged by Psalm 103:2-3, Bless the Lord, O my soul, and forget not all his benefits, Who forgiveth all thine iniquities, who healeth all thy diseases.

Dear Lord, I acknowledge my sin and want to change. Humble me, O God – to know Your will for my life. Amen.

Repentance – New Testament

When Jesus heard it, he saith unto them, "They that are whole have no need of the physician; but they that are sick. I came not to call the righteous, but sinners to repentance."
Mark 2:11

Jesus is still calling sinners to repentance because he loves everyone and wants them spared the punishment of sin.

An American Indian preacher I knew best illustrated repentance.

He walked across the church stage only to stop at the far end.

He said, "Before you go the other way, you must stop. Repentance works the same way: you stop doing wrong, and start doing right."

Then he proceeded to walk back to the center of the stage.

Consider stopping in front of God to acknowledge sin -- then proceed on to righteousness and truth.

Jesus illustrated repentance when he called a little child out of a crowd and said, "Except ye be converted and become as little children, ye shall not enter into the kingdom of heaven," (Matthew 18:3).

Dear Father in Heaven, I know I'm doing wrong and I humble myself before you. Forgive my sin. Allow me to live righteously in Christ Jesus. Amen.

Other Bible References about Repentance: Job 42:6; Psalms 103, 106:45; Luke 13:5-7; John 8:9; Acts 1:5; Hebrews 6:1-6; Revelation 2:5.

Oh, how love I thy law! It is my meditation all the day.
Psalms 119:97

Meditating in the law as the Psalmist does is pleasing to God and will lead to a successful life.

(Consider reading Deuteronomy 6-8 to see how God blesses those people who obey His laws.)

The laws begin in Exodus 20:1-17 – commonly referred to as the Ten Commandments – written by the finger of God on two tablets of stone. Read each commandment with understanding.

The Bible says, Give me understanding, and I shall keep thy law; yea, I shall observe it with my whole heart (Psalms 119:34).

There are more laws in the Book of Leviticus, that refer to human relations, material goods, and sanctification.

The laws had the power to free the Israelites from slavery, but they are also designed to help us find God.

The Bible says, The law of the Lord is perfect, converting the soul; the testimony of the Lord is sure, making wise the simple. The statutes of the Lord are right, rejoicing the heart; the commandment of the Lord is pure, enlightening the eyes (Psalms 19:7-8).

Dear Lord, I thank you for your laws. They guide me in the way I should go. Amen.

There is therefore now no condemnation to them which are in Christ Jesus, who walk not after the flesh, but after the spirit. For the law of the Spirit of life in Christ Jesus hath made me free from the law of sin and death.

Romans 8:1-2

Righteousness in Christ continues to obey the law.

Christ said he did not come to destroy the law, but fulfill it (Matthew 5: 17).

Christ gives an example of acknowledging the law when he healed a man's paralyzed hand on the Sabbath day, but he incorporated mercy in his action (Luke 6:6-10).

Christ said in response to his accusers, "Is it lawful on the Sabbath days to do good, or to do evil; to save life, or destroy it?"

We are to perform righteousness (1 John 3:10).

In fact, we are warned that our righteousness should exceed the righteousness of the scribes and Pharisees (Matthew 5:20).

But Christ knew the religious law of sacrificial offerings could not completely redeem a person from sin, so he fulfilled God's mission for a new testament, providing his body as a sacrifice.

Dear Father, I thank you for the law which helps guide and protect me, but I also thank you for Jesus, who died for my sin and frees me to serve you. Amen.

Other Bible References about Righteousness: Job 35:2; Psalms 37:16, 92:13; Proverbs 13:21; Isaiah 64:6; Romans 3:21-31, 5:18-21; 2 Corinthians 5:2; 1 Peter 2:13-14; Revelation 19:11; Ten Commandments from God: Exodus 20:3-17; Psalm of righteousness, Psalms 119.

And when the morning arose, the angels hastened Lot, saying, Arise, take thy wife, and thy two daughters, the Lord being merciful unto him: and they brought him forth, and set him without the city.

Genesis 19:16

Two angels came into Lot's life to save him and his family from a disaster -- but Lot took his time leaving and the angels had to grab his hand.

When God shows us the way for safety, we should obediently follow. The Bible says, But whoso hearkeneth unto me shall dwell safely, and shall be quiet from fear of evil (Proverbs 1:33).

Lot then complained about going to a mountain the angels said was safe.

Maybe it was too far away, or maybe his family was too tired, but God again had mercy and allowed Lot and family to stop at the town of Zoar.

Lot and his family were saved from the wicked town's burning fire, except for Lot's wife, who disobeyed the angel's command by looking back.

Dear Lord, You are my true refuge, and I turn to you for guidance on being safe. Have mercy on me, my friends, and my family. Amen.

For whosoever shall call upon the name of the Lord shall be saved.

Romans 10:13

One night I called on the Lord for safety, because a terrible fight had broken out among my fellow soldiers in Korea, where I was stationed. Soldiers were beating each other with sticks.

I had no intention of fighting when I was leaving the country in a few weeks, so I sat in the back of a pickup truck in a dark parking lot, praying for safety.

But sometimes, we must be still for safety.

A year earlier, I was sitting in a recreation room with friends when an armed man came in and requested everyone to empty their pockets.

As it turned out, the man said he was joking, but it was a joke that could have turned deadly, because war veterans in the room were ready to retaliate.

Trust the Lord to keep you safe. He is our refuge and fortress, and a present help in time of trouble.

Dear Lord, I trust you to keep me safe. And I trust in Christ, who died for my sins for eternal security. Amen.

Other Bible References about Safety: Psalms Chapters 4, 5, & 6, 118:8-9, 121:7-8, 137:3-5; Proverbs 3:24, 18:10; Micah 7:5; Matthew 10:28; John 14:1-3; 1 Peter 3:12-14; Wisdom protects from fear of evil, Proverbs 1:20-33; Blessedness of trusting God, Psalms 146.

"Truly my soul waiteth upon God; from Him only cometh my salvation."

Psalms 62:1

Another meaning for the word "waiteth" in the Hebrew transliteration is *silence* -- only to God in silence is my soul; from Him only comes my salvation.

Silence and salvation work together.

It was only after the biblical character Job *ended his words* did God fully reveal Himself and grant salvation (Job 31:40-42:5).

Consider being quiet in front of God to find salvation.

That means separating yourself from worldly distractions, confessing sin, and asking forgiveness.

Dear Lord, "Salvation belongeth unto the Lord: thy blessing is upon thy people. Hear me when I call, O God of my righteousness: thou hast enlarged me when I was in distress; have mercy upon me, and hear my prayer" (Psalms 3:8-4:1). Amen.

Salvation – New Testament

That if thou shalt confess with the mouth the Lord Jesus, and shalt believe in thine heart that God hath raised him from the dead, thou shalt be saved.
Romans 10:9

Salvation is available to anyone who calls on the name of the Lord, confesses sin, and accepts Jesus as Savior (Romans 10:11-21).

God is able to give us salvation through Jesus because Jesus was a holy offering of sacrifice.

The sinful rich man Zaccheus received salvation, when he let Jesus into his home. Jesus said, "This day is salvation come to this house," (Luke 19:9).

Christ says, "Behold, I stand at the door, and knock: if any man hear my voice, and open the door, I will come in to him, and will sup with him, and he with me," (Revelation 3:20).

May we open the door of our lives for Jesus to give us salvation.

Dear Lord, I praise you for providing Jesus Christ to take away my sin and give me salvation. Amen.

Other Bible References: Psalms 32, 51; 91; Luke 2:30, Romans 1:16; Hebrews 9:28; 1 John 1:9.

"For thou didst it secretly, but I will do this thing before all Israel, and before the sun."
2 Samuel 12:12

Not only was God going to expose David's sin before the local people, but all over the land.

David had secretly lain with another man's wife, and then placed the man on the front line of a battlefield to be killed.

God knows our secrets, whether they are good or evil.

As the story goes, Nathan the prophet was told by God to confront David about the sin.

If our secrets are good, God may conceal the matter for His glory, such as Joseph withholding his identity from his brothers so they would have grain in time of famine (Genesis 42: 7-9). The biblical man Abraham withheld his identity about being Sarah's husband from King Abimelech to save his life.

But if our secrets are evil, he may expose the matter, because He loves us enough to correct us and put us on the right path.

God's secrets are for a good purpose, when we know God.

Dear Lord, There is nothing hidden before you. I confess my secret sins and agree to live an open righteous life. Amen.

"For nothing is secret that shall not be made manifest, neither anything hid, that shall not be known and come abroad."

Luke 8:17

The Bible also says: All things are indeed open and naked unto Him with whom we have to do (Hebrews 4:13).

So if we have secret sins, we should confess them; then we don't have unnecessary burdens to carry.

But some secrets are to be revealed in God's time, such as when Christ's mother Mary kept the sayings of the shepherds in her heart about the baby Jesus (Luke 2:6-19). (King Herod was seeking to kill infant children; Matthew 2:16.)

But the gift that God gives us in Jesus should be no secret: we should openly proclaim to the world that God has sent a Savior to redeem sin.

Dear Lord, I praise you for taking away my secret sins by confession and the acceptance of Jesus. Now I can live openly and share the gospel that frees other people. Amen.

Other Bible References about Secrets: Deuteronomy 29:29; Proverbs 25:2; Psalms 90:8; Ecclesiastes 12:13; Isaiah 48:16; Matthew 5:14-16; Ephesians 5:11-13.

And it came to pass after these things, that his master's wife cast her eyes upon Joseph; and she said, "Lie with me."
Genesis 39:6

Joseph refused to lay down with his master's wife because it would be a sin against God's law.

When there is a temptation to have illicit sexual relations, invoke God's name for separation; God is a holy God who wants all our attention on him, rather than an inordinate affair.

The Bible advises men to stay away from a strange woman (Proverbs 7:5); lust not after her beauty in thine heart; neither let her take thee with her eyelids (Proverbs 6:25).

God's laws also concerning improper sexual relations with people or animals are in the Book of Leviticus: Chapters 18-20; and regulations for issues that proceed from a man or woman are also in Leviticus, Chapter 15.

If a man does have relations with a woman who is not married, he shall surely endow her to be his wife (Exodus 22:16).

Dear Lord, Thank you for your word that guides me. May I please you, rather than the lust of the flesh. Amen.

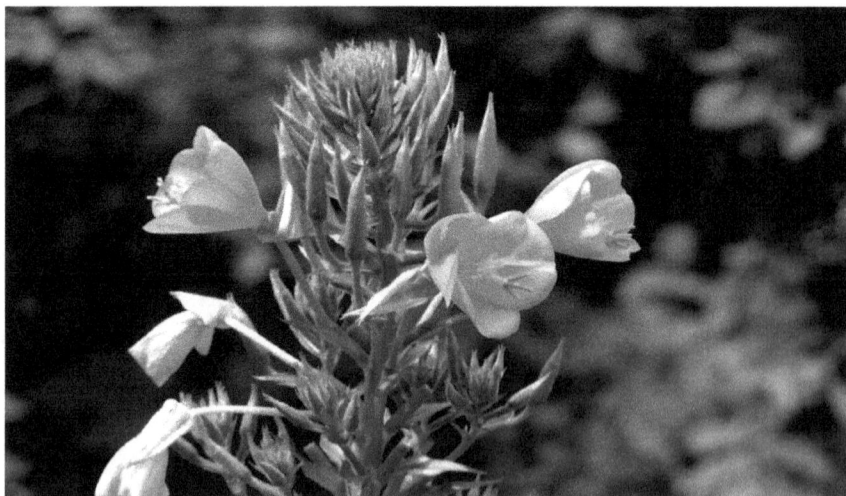

Sex Relations (unmarried) – New Testament

This I say then, "Walk in the Spirit, and ye shall not fulfill the lust of the flesh."
                                                      Galatians 5:16

Walking in the spirit concentrates on such things as peace, humbleness, grace, and righteousness.

But often, the desires of the flesh get in the way.

This is when we need to be humble and call on God for help, and fortunately, Jesus has overcome the desires of the flesh.

When Satan offered him stones turned into bread, at a time when Jesus was hungry, Jesus refused and invoked God's name (Matthew 4:3-4).

Jesus helps us overcome the lust of the flesh and its inordinate desires (Romans 8:3; Galatians 5:17-24).

To avoid fornication, the Bible says it is not good for a man to touch a woman (1 Corinthians 7:1); yet we are advised to let every man have his own wife; and let every woman have her own husband (1 Corinthians 7:2); it is better to marry than to burn (1 Corinthians 7:9).

Dear Lord, I praise you for Christ who has power over the lust of the flesh. I will serve you in the spirit of life that gives you glory. Amen.

Other Bible References about Sex and the Body: Exodus 22:16; Isaiah 52:11; Matthew 19:10-12; Romans 7:4; 1 Corinthians 5:3, 6:13-19, 7:1; Hebrews 13:4; James 2:14-15; 2 Peter 2:9.

And God blessed them, and God said unto them, "Be fruitful, and multiply . . . ."

Genesis 1:28

God commanded Adam and Eve to reproduce, but it was only after they were disciplined in the Garden of Eden, to know each other.

Adam was then sensitive to Eve's weakness and emotions. Eve accepted Adam's strength and leadership.

The Book of Solomon gives a fine example of love between a man and a woman.

The Shulamite bride speaks of her beloved, "My beloved is mine, and I am his: he feedeth among the lilies. Until the day break, and the shadows flee away, turn, my beloved, and be thou like a roe or a young hart upon the mountain of Bether" (Song of Solomon 2:16-17).

And the bridegroom adores his bride: "How fair is thy love, my sister, my spouse! How much better is thy love than wine! And the smell of thine ointments than all spices!" (Song of Solomon 4:10).

Dear Lord, I praise you for my mate. May we nurture each other and enjoy the blessings that come from a commitment to you. Amen.

Sex Relations (married) – New Testament

*Let the husband render unto the wife due benevolence:
and likewise also the wife unto the husband. The wife hath
not power of her own body, but the husband: and likewise
also the husband hath not power of his own body, but the
wife.*

1 Corinthians 7:3-4

Due benevolence recognizes each mate has a yearning to
be physically loved.

There is no greater joy than to please a mate that God
has brought together in marriage.

However, we must be aware of selfish lusts, and the
Apostle Paul has given us some advice: Defraud ye not one
the other, except it be with consent for a time, that ye may
give yourselves to fasting and prayer; and come together
again, that Satan tempt you not for your incontinency (1
Cor. 7:5).

Advice in the Book of Ephesians helps keep marriages in
the right place: Husbands, love your wives, even as Christ
also loved the church, and gave himself for it (Ephesians
5:25). Wives submit yourselves unto your own husbands as
unto the Lord (Ephesians 5:22).

Men might be reminded they are to give honor unto the
wife, as unto the weaker vessel -- that their prayers be not
hindered (1 Peter 3:7).

Marriage is honorable in all, and the bed undefiled
(Hebrews 13:4).

*Dear Father in Heaven, Thank you so much for my
spouse. May I be sensitive to my mate's needs and you in the
spirit. Amen.*

Sickness – Old Testament

And the Lord will take away from thee all sickness . . . .
Deuteronomy 7:15

The Lord takes away sicknesses by obedience to His commandments in the Book of Deuteronomy, but many of us think going to a doctor, taking drugs, or learning psychology will make us well.

Only a pure and holy God can heal, and purging of sin begins the healing process.

In Isaiah's time, prideful King Hezekiah was sick unto death, but Hezekiah separated himself to God and prayed (Isaiah 38): Hezekiah's sins were cast away (Isaiah 38:17), and he was made whole. Hezekiah also used a natural remedy of boiled figs (2 Kings 20:7).

The true God says, "I wound, and I heal" (Deuteronomy 32:39).

It's up to us to find God's healing, which takes obedience and faith.

Consider reading also Isaiah 56-58 to separate yourself to God and become a whole person free of disease.

Dear Lord, I thank you for showing me how to become well by separating myself to you in complete obedience. I trust you and your provisions to make me well. Amen

Sickness – New Testament

For we have not a high priest which cannot be touched with the feeling of our infirmities; but was in all points tempted like as we are yet without sin. Let us therefore come boldly unto the throne of grace, that we may obtain mercy, and find grace in time of need.
Hebrews 4:14-16

Christ can help heal us because he is holy and sits on the right hand of God. Further, he has purged our sins by taking them to the cross.

A woman, who had an issue of blood for twelve years that no doctor could heal, reached out and touched Jesus and was made whole (Mark 5:25-34).

Touching Jesus in the heavens makes us whole.

When infection comes, look to Christ for purity.

When wounded, look to Christ to bind up.

And when apathy comes, look to Christ for strength and resurrection.

Belief and faith in the risen Christ heals.

Dear Lord, I humble myself before you and praise you for Jesus Christ who takes away my sin. Grant me the strength I need to glorify and praise you. Amen.

Other Bible References about Healing: Exodus 23:25; Psalms 103:1-4; Proverbs 17:22; 24:10; Isaiah 35:3, 52:4;, 57:14, 58:8-9; Jeremiah 17:14; Matthew 4:23-24, 11:28-30; Luke 9:1; James 5:16.

For Achan . . . of the tribe of Judah . . . took of the accursed thing: and the anger of the Lord was kindled against the children of Israel.

Joshua 7:1

The sin of one man caused a lot of trouble for the Israel army.

God had commanded the army to not take any goods when they defeated the king of Jericho, but soldier Achan took and hid some.

In the next battle, Israel was defeated, for sin was in the camp.

When there is sin in our lives, it destroys us.

A burden is constantly on our minds, and we no longer give attention to work details. We make mistakes.

Failure to acknowledge sin compounds them. And God is not with us.

Before confidence can be restored, sin must be confessed and abandoned.

Though Achan did this, it was too late to receive mercy, and he was slain.

A psalmist's prayer helps us avoid future sin: Keep back thy servant also from presumptuous sins; let them not have dominion over me . . . (Psalm 19:13).

We might also take Solomon's advice in the Book of Proverbs: He that covereth his sins shall not prosper but whoso confesseth and forsaketh them, shall have mercy (Proverbs 28:13).

Dear Lord, I am sorry that I have sinned. Please take away my sins and grant me mercy. I am willing to recompense that which I have caused suffering. Amen.

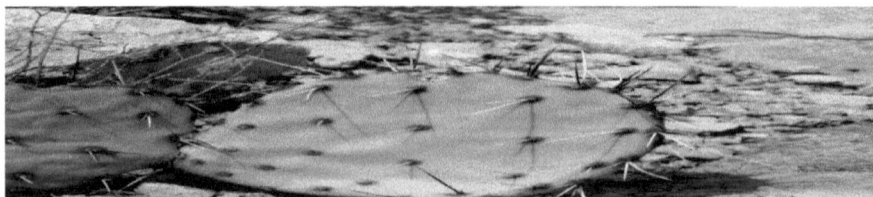

Sin – New Testament

What shall we say then? Is the law sin? Nay, I had not known sin but by the law; for I had not known lust, except the law had said, Thou shalt not covet.

Romans 7:7

The Apostle Paul admonishes his knowledge of the law because it brought him to know sin.

Sin is a transgression of the law that brings punishment, but we have Christ as a sacrifice for our sin, if we are remorseful and confess sin in front of merciful God.

If we say we have no sin, we make a God a liar (1 John 1:10). All men have sinned and have come short of the glory of God (Romans 3:23).

Sin causes us and other people to suffer, but it helps us to know God loves whom he corrects, and we should be open to His discipline (Hebrews 12:8-11).

Dear Lord, I acknowledge my sin. Have mercy on me by Christ Jesus who died for my sin. Forgive me and I shall be forgiven, and I will testify of your salvation and mercy forever. Amen.

Other Bible References about Sin: Numbers 32:23; Psalms 25:6, 51:1-4, Isaiah 53:6; Ezekiel 36:25-26; Acts 10:43; Romans 6:11, 10:8; 2 Corinthians 5:17-18; I John 2:1-2; 3:5; Hebrews 10:14; 1 Peter 2:24.

I have stuck unto thy testimonies; O Lord, put me not to shame. I will run the way of thy commandments, when thou shalt enlarge my heart.

Psalms 119:31-32

Other than men warring, people rising up to play around a golden calf, and the strong man Samson being paraded by the lords of the Philistines, sporting of the physical body is non-existent in the Bible.

Our bodies are to be used for His service, such as nursing the sick, feeding the poor, and sheltering the homeless.

God has said, Thou shalt have no other god's before me (Exodus 20:3), and that would include balls, goal posts, nets, and fences.

We are not to bow down nor worship false gods, who cannot think, see, or hear (Exodus 20:5; Daniel 5:23).

God is our true bread for life.

Dear Father in Heaven, May this body be used for your humble service. I bow and worship before you in holiness and truth. Amen.

Know ye not that they who run in a race run all, but one receiveth the prize? So run, that ye may obtain. Now every man that striveth for the mastery is temperate in all things. Now they do it to obtain a corruptible crown, but we, an incorruptible.

1 Corinthians 9:24-25

Receiving a trophy in sports competition for successfully finishing above other competitors is a great feeling, but receiving a crown of glory from God through Jesus Christ for the gift of eternal life is the best prize of all: it never deteriorates.

Our bodies are to be used for God's glory (1 Corinthians 6:19-20). Constructing housing for the homeless, cooking for the hungry, and transporting the disabled are just a few ways to witness and testify for God, but if we are sporting them for personal recognition, we are not glorifying God.

God may cause us to suffer injury or defeat -- to know he is God.

The Bible says, For bodily exercise profiteth little: but godliness is profitable unto all things . . . (1 Timothy 4:8).

Dear Lord, May my body be used for your purpose and glory. Have mercy upon me. Amen.

Strength – Old Testament

And Samson lay till midnight, and arose at midnight, and took the doors of the gate of the city, and the two posts, and went away with them, bar and all, and put them upon his shoulders, and carried them up to the top of a hill that is before Hebron.

Judges 16:3

Samson was a physically strong man carrying the front gate materials up a hill. (He had also torn a lion in pieces, caught 300 foxes, and slayed a thousand Philistines.)

But spiritually, Samson was weak. He told his girlfriend Delilah the secret of his strength. She told the lords of the Philistines who hired men to come and shave Samson's holy hair (Numbers 6:1). And Samson was imprisoned.

By God, we receive strength (Psalms 68:34-35), but if we have turned away from God, we have lost our strength.

David the psalmist said, My strength faileth because of mine iniquity (Psalms 31:10).

Confessing our sins and coming into agreement with God will nourish us back to strength.

Be reminded there was not one feeble person among the Israelites who came into the land of God's promise (Psalms 105:37).

Seek the Lord and His strength: seek His face evermore (Psalms 105:4). However, if thou faint in the day of adversity, thy strength is small (Proverbs 24:10).

Dear Lord, Feed me the food which makes me strong, yet feed me your word which makes me wise unto salvation and life. Amen.

Strength – New Testament

I can do all things with Christ who strengtheneth me.
Philippians 4:13

Christ gives us strength because he can take away our sins.

In different words, he can take away the troubles that burden our bodies and minds and give us strength to work for God in the Spirit.

Yet we do pray for God to give us our daily bread, and eating a good meal gives us physical strength to work for God. (For one believeth that he may eat all things: another, who is weak, eateth herbs; Romans 14:2).

The Apostle Paul said he would rather be weak, because it brought him to closer to God: "Therefore, I take pleasure in infirmities, in reproaches, in necessities, in persecutions, in distresses for Christ's sake: for when I am weak, then am I strong"(2 Corinthians 12:9-10).

When Paul was experiencing pain, the Lord gave him a message, "My grace is sufficient for thee; for my strength is made perfect in weakness (2 Corinthians 12: 9).

Dear Father in Heaven. I thank you for the strength in Christ Jesus who is risen and inspires me to become stronger. I also thank you for removing a burden of sin by my confession and humbleness. Amen.

Other Bible References: Leviticus 26:40; Psalms 22:26, 37:26, 71:16, 84:5; Proverbs 18:10, 24:10; Matthew 4:4; Luke 2:40; Ephesians 3:16, 6:10; Hebrews 8:10; Sin saps strength, Psalms 31:10.

Stress – Old Testament

And it came to pass on the morrow, that Moses sat to judge the people: and the people stood by Moses from the morning to evening.

Exodus 18:13

Moses was experiencing a lot of stress judging all the affairs of the people; his father-in-law gave him some advice to appoint some more judges.

We may have to let go of pride and seek alternative help when experiencing stress; otherwise, we may suffer physical and mental exhaustion.

Consider reading Psalm 107, which shows the children of Israel suffering from stress: they were overworked, wandering, confused, and sinful; yet the psalmist extolled God's goodness and mercy.

Dear Lord, Have mercy on me and forgive me for being so prideful. You are my first desire, and I lay down my pride to accept Your will for my life. Amen.

"Come unto me, all ye that labor and are heavy laden, and I will give you rest. Take my yoke upon you, and learn of me: for I am meek and lowly in heart: and ye shall find rest unto your souls. For my yoke is easy, and my burden is light."

Matthew 11:28-30

Jesus' burden was light because he had no sin.

His yoke was easy because it was attached to his Father in Heaven who gave him grace and comfort. .

The Comforter is sent to all of us believers who decide to give up personal ambition and accept Jesus Christ as Savior. Pride, selfishness, and fighting are given up.

The scriptures encourage us to cease from our *own* work, as God did from his -- from the foundation of the world (read Hebrews 4:10).

Consider this man Jesus, who made himself of no reputation, and took upon him the form of a servant (Philippians 2:7).

He gives us rest from stress and freedom from sin.

Dear Lord, I praise You for Jesus who takes away my sin to give me rest. Have mercy upon me. Amen.

Other Bible References: Romans 9:16; Galatians 6:5.

See, I have set before thee this day, life and good, and death and evil.
Deuteronomy 30:15

Moses put a choice of life and death before the people to test their faith.

God puts the same choice before us at some time in life..

If we choose life, we testify of God's saving presence and glory, but if we choose death, we cannot praise God from the grave (Psalms 6:5; 88:10).

Serving God will keep us alive but we must make a true commitment.

Commander Joshua later gave the people an ultimatum: "And if seem evil to you to serve the Lord, choose you this day whom ye will serve" (Joshua 24:15).

The people responded, "The Lord our God will we serve, and his voice will we obey" (Joshua 24:24).

God commands us not to kill (Exodus 20:13), and that includes us as well as other people.

Dear Lord, "For thou hast delivered my soul from death; mine eyes from tears, and my feet from falling. I will walk before the Lord in the land of the living" (Psalms 116:8-9). Amen.

Suicide – New Testament

"For God so loved the world that he gave his only begotten Son, that whosoever believeth in him should not perish, but have everlasting life."
John 3:16

Christ has already died for us – so we can live.

But it often takes a near death experience until we call on him.

The Apostle Paul thought of dying when he was troubled, yet he did not trust in himself, but trusted in God for help (2 Corinthians 1:8-9).

Christ Jesus gives us power over death (1 Corinthians 15:54-57). The last enemy death has been defeated, by Christ's resurrection from the grave.

May we give up selfish desires and hold onto the living Christ -- to serve God in the spirit.

He is risen, and we can be risen with him by belief.

Dear Lord, I humbly accept Christ by the confession of sin. I am renewed in the spirit of my mind to live for You. For whosoever shall call upon the name of the Lord shall be saved (Romans 10:13). Amen.

Other Bible References: Genesis 3:22; Deuteronomy 4:1; Job 2:6; Psalms 16:11, 27:1, 34:6, 118:17-18; Isaiah 42:7; John 10:10, 11:25, 16:33; Romans 10:13; Ephesians 4:8-10; Hebrews 12:9.

Terror – Old Testament

And Mount Sinai was altogether on a smoke, because the Lord descended upon it in fire: and the smoke thereof ascended as the smoke of a furnace, and the whole mount quaked greatly.

Exodus 19:18

God shook the earth, flooded the valley, and made thundering noises in the sky. The people were scared of these events, so their leader Moses told them to get back -- only Aaron the priest and Moses could proceed to look at God's terror.

When powerful events happen, look to God for direction. God can be a consuming fire, yet he will warn us when catastrophic events are about to happen.

Moses comforted the people and said God was testing their faith -- to see if they would fear him.

Dear Lord, I know you are a mighty God and worthy to be feared. Have mercy upon me as I draw close to you and seek your will. Amen.

"For nation shall rise against nation, and kingdom against kingdom; and there shall be famines, pestilences, and earthquakes in divers places."

Matthew 24:7

Jesus says terrible events may end the world and mankind, so he warns us to be prepared, such as five brides waiting to see their bridegroom in the dark: the brides had their oil ready to burn for the lamps to shine (Matthew 25:1-13).

The advent of terrifying events makes us want to be prepared for God to save us.

Jesus comforts us saying he will be in the midst of terror -- in the clouds of heaven with great power and glory (Matthew 24:31).

Take comfort in knowing, that there is nothing that has happened, that has not happened before (1 Peter 4:12).

We are not to be scared of man's terror, who can kill the body (1 Peter 3:14); but we are to fear God, who can destroy body and soul in hell (Matthew 10:28).

Jesus has promised to be with us to the end (Matthew 28:20).

Dear Lord, I thank you for Jesus in my life. I know I have safety in heaven regardless of what happens in the world. Jesus has prepared a place for me. Establish peace I pray, all over the world. Amen.

Other Bible References: Psalms 65, 68, 91:5-6; Joel 2:10-11.

Oh, give thanks unto the Lord, for he is good; for his mercy endureth forever.

Psalms 136:1

God is worthy to be thanked because he gives us peace and mercy.

We might return thanks by offering the first profits from our investments, serving the public, or performing good deeds for neighbors.

But the greatest thanks we can give is dedicating our life to him.

The Bible says, Offer unto God thanksgiving, and pay thy vows unto the Most High, and call upon me in the day of trouble; I will deliver thee, and thou shalt glorify me (Psalms 50:14-15).

King David gave his life to God and said a lengthy prayer that thanked him (I Chronicles 16:7-36).

If we do not acknowledge God, nor thank him, he may not acknowledge us (2 Chronicles 15:2).

Dear Lord, I thank you for your presence here and praise your holy name. You are good and your mercy endures forever. Amen.

Thankfulness – New Testament

Giving thanks always for all things unto God and the Father in the name of our Lord Jesus Christ.
Ephesians 5:20

Thank God for providing a Savior in the person of Jesus Christ to take away our sins and give us everlasting life!

Not only are we to share and worship Christ with other believers, but we are to go to the lost, sick, and homeless.

Jesus said, "For if ye love them who love you, what thanks have ye? For sinners also love those who love them. And if ye do good to them who do good to you, what thanks have ye? For sinners also do even the same" (Luke 6:32-33).

Feeding the poor, nursing the impoverished, and sharing God's word with young people are ways to receive thanks.

While we perform good deeds for the needy (James 1:22-25), may we continue to give the sacrifice of praise to God continually, that is the fruit of *our* lips giving thanks (Hebrews 13:15).

Dear Lord, Thank you for Jesus who died for me so that I can serve you. May I give thanks everyday in my words, tithes, and deeds. Amen.

Other Bible References: 1 Chronicles 16:8; Psalms 35:18;, 66, 75:1, 95:2, 100:4-5; 1 Corinthians 15:57; Colossians 3:1; Philippians 4:6.

"... For the Lord thy God is with thee whithersoever thou goest."

Joshua 1:9

Joshua received these words from God shortly before leading his people into a strange land.

Knowing God is with us gives us courage to travel, not only in times of danger, but it time of leisure.

However, we are warned that the sight [from] the eyes is better than the wandering of the desire (Ecclesiastes 6:9). We can enjoy God's presence right here in prayer and fellowship.

But if we have to travel, may we look to God for guidance.

He will lead us in righteousness.

He will comfort, feed, and protect us, but we must call on His name for guidance and be at peace with him.

Dear Lord, I thank you for being here and in my destination. Provide me with necessary provisions and keep me safe. Amen.

And it came to pass, afterward, that he went throughout every city and village, preaching and showing the glad tidings of the kingdom of God; and the twelve were with him.

Luke 8:1

Jesus did a lot of traveling witnessing for God.

He also encountered a lot of delays. He met people with demons and illnesses. Lawyers, soldiers, and priests asked him questions. And he had to avoid people who were trying to hurt him.

But Jesus was on a mission to bring good tidings to the people. He would feed people with bread, heal the sick, and teach people the oracles of God.

When we travel, we should be so compassionate towards other people, and express God's love.

The Bible says to forbear one another in love (Ephesians 4:2; Colossians 3:13).

May we prepare in advance for travel by acquiring necessary provisions, but also gather material to witness for God and Christ.

The love for Jesus transcends all people and cultures.

Dear Father, Your word of life is commissioned to be spread all over the world. May everyone know about Jesus. Have mercy on me when I travel. Amen.

Other Bible References about Travel: Psalms 23; Proverbs 27:8; Matthew 10:9-10; 28:19; John 14:2-3,23; Hebrews 13:5.

But he knoweth the way that I take: when he hath tried me, I shall come forth as gold. My foot hath held his steps, his way have I kept, and not declined.

Job 23:10-11

Job stayed around God's throne regardless of personal trouble.

We should be so faithful when troubles come; we do not want to doubt the plan God has for our lives (read Psalms 78 and 95).

Other saints of God were as faithful as Job.

Abraham was about to sacrifice his son on an altar, but by obedience to God, he found an animal sacrifice (Genesis 22: 1-14).

Daniel was put in a den of lions, but he kept his faith in God for safety (Daniel 6:16-23).

Life is full of trials that test our faith, but at the end of the journey, he will fulfill the promise.

Dear Father in Heaven, I praise you for being here and saving me from sin. You have control over this situation, and I praise you for keeping me humble and righteous. Amen.

That the trial of your faith, being much more precious than of gold that perisheth, though it be tried with fire, might be found unto praise and honor and glory at the appearing of Jesus Christ.

1 Peter 1:7

Our faith in God is confronted with temptations to sin, but trusting in Jesus and reading the Scriptures helps us overcome temptation.

When Jesus was faced with temptation, he rejected it and quoted scripture: Thou shalt not tempt the Lord, thy God (Matthew 4:7).

The concordances in most Bibles provide reference Scriptures for words about temptation.

Researching those words and reading scriptures will find that God has victory over a personal temptation to commit evil.

The Bible says, My brethren, count it all joy when ye fall into divers temptations, Knowing this, that the trying of your faith worketh patience (James 1:2-3).

Dear Lord, Thank you for Your Son Jesus, who has victory over evil. May I follow the plan you have for my life that is good and gives you glory. Amen.

Truth – Old Testament

God is not a man that he should lie; neither the son of man that he should repent. Hath he said and shall he not do it? Or hath he spoken and shall he not make it good?
Numbers 23:19

God can be trusted because he fulfills obligations.

Man cannot be trusted because he cannot always fulfill promises.

Therefore, we should look to God for truth.

Deuteronomy 32:4 says he is the rock, his work is perfect; for all his ways are judgment; a God of truth and without iniquity, just and right is he.

And the Psalmist praised this God of truth: Thy righteousness is an everlasting righteousness, and thy law is the truth (Psalms 119:142).

We need this God of truth, because we are prone to sin and wander aimlessly.

King David's prayer gives us a good example to follow: Lead me in thy truth, teach me, for thou art the God of my salvation, on thee do I wait all the day (Psalms 25:5).

God has provided us truth in the Holy Scriptures. It's up to us to search it out and hold onto it.

All the paths of the Lord are mercy and truth unto such as keep his covenant and his testimonies (Psalm 25:10).

Dear Lord, I thank you for providing your record of truth in the Old Testament. Your word is truly a lamp unto my feet and a light unto my path. Amen.

Jesus saith unto him, I am the way, the truth, and the life . . . .

John 14:6

Truth records that the Gentiles needed a Savior, so God sent His son Jesus in the form and lineage of the first man Adam to be a sacrifice for the sins of the people.

Jesus was born of a virgin woman, died for the people's sins, and rose into heaven on the third day. He now intercedes on behalf of believers to comfort and encourage them.

Men who refuse the teachings and acceptance of Christ as Savior are referred to as anti-Christs (false Christs, 1 John 4:1-3).

This is the beginning of finding truth:

Man is prone to make errors and needs a divine Savior like Jesus for sanctification. (If we say we have not sinned, we make God a liar; 1 John 1:10.)

According to Jesus, those who worship God are to worship in spirit and truth (John 4:24); but Jesus also says, "No man cometh to the Father but by me" (John 14:26).

Upon confession of Jesus, God sends us the Spirit of truth (John 14:17, 15-26-27, 16:13).

Dear Lord, I praise You for the truth that comes by Jesus. Forgive my sins and sanctify me by this truth. Amen.

Other Bible References: Deuteronomy 11:16; Psalms 25:5, 31:5, 119:151,160; John 3:11, 4:24, 8:14-18, 16:13; 2 Timothy 2:11; Hebrews 6:18; 1 John 4:6; True light from God sent from John the Baptist, John 1: 18.

War – Old Testament

The Lord is a man of war; the Lord is his name.
Exodus 15:3

This was the statement exclaimed by Moses after the Lord had drowned Pharaoh's men and chariots into the Red Sea – while the children of Israel crossed to the other side.

God avenged His people of oppression; he created havoc to free the people to worship him.

But many of us war for land, money, natural resources, or to enslave people.

We are warned in God's law not to covet anything from a neighbor (Exodus 20:17), nor oppress strangers (Exodus 22:21).

Violations of these precepts often lead to war and defeat. We are to rebuke a person in righteousness (Leviticus 19:17).

But often the war is within ourselves: one part of us wants to do one thing, while the other wants to do the opposite.

May we humble ourselves from personal war and seek the peace that comes from God by confession of sin and obedience to the law.

God creates war, but he also makes war to cease (Psalms 46:9).

Dear Lord, You are in charge of war, and your righteousness and glory will prevail. May the people be spared of violence to worship you and bow down before You. Amen.

Then said Jesus unto him, "Put up again thy sword into its place; for all they that take up the sword perish by the sword."

Matthew 26:52

Christ gives us wisdom and says if we use weapons, they will be used against us.

But Christ does make war. According to the author of the Book of Revelation, he wars from heaven in righteousness (Revelation 19:11).

The soldier Saul became a victim of Christ when he was riding down the road and brought to a stop (Acts 9:1-20).

Christ asked Saul why he was persecuting him.

Humiliated and partly disabled, Saul was led into the city of Damascus where he received instructions from the disciple Ananias to go and preach about Jesus.

The war continues to spread the good news about Jesus.

For he is our peace, who hath made both one, and hath broken down the middle wall of partition between us (Ephesians 2:14).

Dear Lord, Thank you for Jesus who has overcome the lust of the flesh and the war within. He allows me to love all of humanity. May I refrain from arguing and fighting and seek this peace that passes all understanding. Amen.

Other Bible References: Deuteronomy 20; Proverbs 20:18; James 4:1; 1 Peter 2:11, 3:10-11.

The fear of the Lord is the beginning of wisdom, but fools despise knowledge and instruction.

Proverbs 1:7

Fearing God is the beginning of wisdom because he has power over our souls. Understanding he is the great teacher, puts us in the right place to learn, for with the lowly is wisdom (Proverbs 11:2).

The wisdom books of the Bible are considered to be Job, Psalms, Proverbs, Ecclesiastes, and the Song of Solomon. The characteristics of wisdom are listed in Proverbs 1-9.

God's wisdom saved Abraham from Melchizedek's army, got Joseph out of jail, taught Jacob how to multiply cattle, helped Noah build an ark, and Nehemiah to rebuild temple walls.

We are encouraged to seek wisdom while it may be found; otherwise, we are warned, God will not answer us when anguish and distress come (Proverbs 1:24-32).

Dear Lord, You have the wisdom, and I humble myself from my own wisdom, to listen to you for discernment, prosperity, and safety. Amen.

Wisdom – New Testament

For the wisdom of this world is foolishness with God. For it is written, He taketh the wise in their own craftiness.
1 Corinthians 3:19

Man would have you believe wisdom comes from worldly textbooks and personal thought, but the Lord knoweth the thoughts of the wise, that they are vain (1 Corinthians 3:20). Wisdom of this world is earthly, sensual, and devilish (James 3:15).

The mystery of receiving great wisdom is explained in the 2nd Chapter of 1 Corinthians: Now we have received not the spirit of the world, but the spirit which is of God . . . (1 Corinthians 2:12).

If any of you lack wisdom, let him ask of God, that giveth to all *men* liberally, and upbraideth not; and it shall be given him (James 1:5). The wisdom that comes from above is first pure, then peaceable . . . (James 3:17).

This is the wisdom we need, which profits us spiritually to have peace.

The greatest wisdom we can have is that which grants personal salvation (2 Timothy 3:15).

Dear Lord, I thank you for wisdom in the Holy Scriptures. Wisdom shows me how to live and receive your blessings, but the greatest wisdom I can have is receiving your Son Jesus who saves my soul. Amen.

Other Bible References: Proverbs 2:6, 8:17, 23:4; Ecclesiastes 1:18; 1 Corinthians 1:19; Colossians 2:3; James 1:5; 1 Timothy 2:15.

Work – Old Testament

And the Lord took the man, and put him into the garden of Eden, to dress it, and to till it.

Genesis 2:15

Man was put on earth to freely work and multiply, but he disobeyed God's command by eating from a tree of knowledge of good and evil; he was condemned to work by the sweat of his face (Genesis 3:17-19).

Nevertheless, the Bible says it is a gift from God to work: There is nothing better for a man . . . that he should make his soul enjoy good in his labor (Ecclesiastes 2:24).

The first job we have on earth is to know the true God, by studying the law, ordinances, and commandments; then we know whom we are working for, and what to produce. (Otherwise, we may be enslaved to another god; read Deuteronomy 4:23-28.)

If we don't want to work, the Bible says we may hunger (Proverbs 19:15).

More wisdom from the Book of Proverbs states: Labor not to be rich; cease from thine own wisdom (Proverbs 23:4); but in all labor, there is profit (Proverbs 14:23).

Dear Lord, I praise You for letting me work. Perfect the work that You have begun in me to produce good things, and may all this work glorify You. Amen.

Work – New Testament

"Labor not for the food which perisheth but for that food which endureth to everlasting life, which the Son of man shall give unto you; for him hath God the Father sealed."
John 6:27

Christ advises us to work for those things which give everlasting life.

When we are pleasing God with work, then daily provisions take care of themselves.

For example, when seventy servants went out to work to spread the good news of salvation, they carried neither purse, money, or shoes; yet they were sustained with daily provisions and returned with joy (Luke 10:4-17).

But the disciples also asked, "What shall we do, that we might work the works of God?"

Jesus answered and said unto them, "This is the work of God, that ye might believe on him whom he hath sent" (John 6:29).

Believing in Jesus gives us access to God's works: we have the power of healing, teaching, nursing, ministering, constructing, and miracles.

Dear Lord, I praise You for showing me the work You want me to do. Perfect that which concerns me, and may Your work prosper. Amen.

Other Bible References about Work: Genesis 3:19; 2 Chronicles 15:7; Psalms 111:2; 138:8; Proverbs 10:4-5; 16:3; 21:25; Ecclesiastes 2:4-7; 9:10; Luke 2:49; John 15:4-5; Galatians 2:16; 6:4; Ephesians 2:8-10; 4:1; Philippians 1:6; 4:13; 2 Thessalonians 3:10-12; James 2:14-26

God is our refuge and strength, a very present help in trouble. Therefore, will not we fear; though the earth be removed, and the mountains carried into the midst of the sea.

Psalms 46:1-2

Psalm 46 comforts us because it shows God is in control regardless of what happens on earth, but there is more wisdom to relieve our worries.

We are not to worry about the next day (Proverbs 27:1). We are not to worry about the weather (Ecclesiastes 11:4). We do not to worry about other countries, for he ruleth by his power forever; his eyes behold the nations (Psalms 66:7). Neither are we to worry about man (Psalms 56:4).

But we have plenty to worry about if we do not know God. The sinner David said of his sin, "I am troubled; I am bowed down greatly; I go mourning all the day long" (Psalm 38:6).

We do not want to be troubled like David, so let's make sure sin is confessed for mercy and life (Proverbs 28:15).

The Psalmist finishes Psalm 46 saying, Be still, and know that I am God . . . (verse 10).

Dear Lord, With You as comforter, I can face this anxiety and feel calm. May I patiently seek this cause for worry and have it removed, for I am saved by faith and trust in You. Amen.

Worry – New Testament

*"Therefore, take no thought saying, What shall we eat?
or, What shall we drink? or, with what shall we be clothed?"*
Matthew 6:31

Much of our worry is about food, drink, or clothing, but Jesus encourages us to trust in God for these provisions. We are to seek the kingdom of God and His righteousness, and daily provisions will be given to us.

Other events may cause us to worry: nearby wars, technological hazards, environmental pollution, or illness.

But God has control over these issues. The world is subject to God (Revelation 14:7); and man is subject to Christ (1 Peter 3:22).

If we know both God and Christ, we will not worry.

The Apostle Paul gives us some advice by saying to be {anxious} for nothing, but in everything, by prayer and supplication with thanksgiving, let your requests be made known unto God (Philippians 4:6).

And the peace of God, which passeth all understanding, shall keep your hearts and mind through Christ Jesus (verse 7).

Dear Lord, Thank you for increasing my faith. I know that You are in control of this situation, and I look to You for the right thing to do. Amen.

Other Bible References: 1 Peter 5:10

Worship – Old Testament

"Thou shalt have no other gods before me. Thou shalt not make unto thee any graven image, or any likeness of anything that is in heaven above, or that is in the earth beneath, or that is in the water under the earth; Thou shalt not bow down thyself to them, nor serve them . . . ."

Exodus 20:3-5

God tells us by His first commandment that he has priority over all other gods, and rightly so: he is able to forgive and redeem sin, grant prosperity or poverty, and give good or bad health.

So he wants worship, and we are commanded to love him with all [our] heart, and with all [our] soul, and with all [our] might (Deuteronomy 6:5).

Psalms 95 exhorts us to worship: O come, let us worship and bow down: let us kneel before the Lord our maker. For he is our God; and we are the sheep of His pasture . . . (verse 5-6).

When the patriarch Jacob and company went to worship God at Bethel, they were to put away their strange gods and get cleaned up (Genesis 35).

That's what we need to do: put away strange gods and get cleaned up. God is holy, and we are to be holy with him. And wherever God wants us to worship, we are to worship him in spirit and truth.

Dear Lord, My praise shall be of thee in the great congregation: I will pay my vows before them that fear him. The meek shall eat and be satisfied: they shall praise the Lord that seek him; your heart shall live forever; (Psalms 22:25-26). Amen.

Worship – New Testament

Blessing, and honor, and glory, and power be unto him that sitteth upon the throne, and unto the Lamb forever and ever.

Revelation 5:13

Jesus is worthy to be worshipped because he is the Son of God who arose from the dead and gives us victory over the fear of death. He sits in the heavens on the right hand of God to intercede for us.

The Bible says, but this man, because he continueth forever . . . is also able to save them to the uttermost that come unto God by him, seeing he ever liveth to make intercession for them (Hebrews 7:24-25).

Christ is at the door to the temple of God in heaven, and if we hear his voice and open the door, he will come in and dine with us (Revelation 3:20).

Dear Lord, I praise You for Jesus in the congregation of saints. You have provided a great sacrifice for our sins. Amen.

Other Bible References about Worshipping: Psalms 22:25-26; 95:6; 138:2; Ecclesiastes 5:1-2; Daniel 5:23; Matthew 25:33-34; John 3:3; 4:23-24; Acts 7:48-49; 1 Corinthians 3:16; Colossians 2:8-9